THE EXPLORATION OF THE
INNER WOUNDS—*HAN*

American Academy of Religion
Academy Series

edited by
Susan Thistlethwaite

Number 86
THE EXPLORATION OF THE
INNER WOUNDS—*HAN*

by
Jae Hoon Lee

Jae Hoon Lee

THE EXPLORATION OF THE INNER WOUNDS—*HAN*

Scholars Press
Atlanta, Georgia

THE EXPLORATION OF THE
INNER WOUNDS—*HAN*

by
Jae Hoon Lee

© 1994
The American Academy of Religion

Library of Congress Cataloging in Publication Data
Lee, Jae Hoon.
    The exploration of the inner wounds-Han / Jae Hoon Lee.
        p. cm. — (American Academy of Religion academy series ; 86)
    Includes bibliographical references.
    ISBN 1-55540-961-X. — ISBN 1-55540-962-8 (pbk.)
    1. Han (Psychology) 2. Sin. 3. Shamanism—Korea. 4. Minjung
theology. 5. Emotions—Religious aspects. I. Title. II. Series.
BF575.H26L44   1994
152.4'09519—dc20   94-2375
                                                            CIP

Printed in the United States of America
on acid-free paper

Acknowledgments

Grateful acknowledgment is made to the following individuals. To Dr. Ann Belford Ulanov for her kind teachings and steadfast support. To Dr. Susan Brooks Thistlethwaite and Dr. Robert J. Hauck for their valuable services as the editor and coordinator of the academy series of AAR.

To John Harlow, Ki-Chang Song, and Myung-Ho Moon for their help in preparing the manuscripts.

CONTENTS

Acknowledgments

Chapter I. Introduction/1

Chapter II. A review of the studies of *han* in Korea/11
 1. Folklore study
   (1) Repressed sexual libido
   (2) The Korean complex
 2. Korean Shamanism
   (1) Deep wounds
   (2) Frustrated wish for eternity
 3. Korean literature: "jeong-han" vs. "wonhan"
 4. Psychological study
   (1) Unlived life
   (2) Negative mother complex
   (3) Split-off part of the ego
   (4) Split infantile mother imago
 5. The original and the secondary *han*

Chapter III. The inner dynamics of the original *han*/27
 1. Melanie Klein and child analysis
 2. Melanie Klein's theory of anxiety
   (1) Persecutory anxiety
   (2) Depressive anxiety
 3. Anxiety and *han*
   (1) Persecutory anxiety and "wonhan"
   (2) Depressive anxiety and "jeong-han"

4. Two position theory
    (1) The paranoid-schizoid position
    (2) The depressive position
5. Three position theory and *han*
    (1) The paranoid position and "wonhan"
    (2) The depressive position and "jeong-han"
    (3) The schizoid position and "huhan"
6. Envy and *han*

Chapter IV. The *han* of three individuals/57
1. King Yonsan and "wonhan"
    (1) Historical records of King Yonsan's *han*
    (2) The inner dynamics of King Yonsan's "wonhan"
        A. Oedipus complex
        B. Persecutory fears
        C. Fragmented ego-objects
        D. Splitting
        E. Projective identification
    (3) The aetiology of King Yonsan's "wonhan"
2. Sowol and "jeong-han"
    (1) Sowol's poetic images of *han*
    (2) The inner dynamics of Sowol's "jeong-han"
    (3) The aetiology of Sowol's "jeong-han"
3. Eun Ko and "huhan"
    (1) The fantasy world of Eun Ko's "huhan"
    (2) The inner dynamics of Eun Ko's "huhan"
    (3) The aetiology of Eun Ko's "huhan"
    (4) The transformation of Eun Ko's "huhan"
    (5) Social implication of "huhan"

Chapter V. The *han* in the symbolism of Korean Shamanism/97
1. The Barikongjoo myth and *han*
    (1) The Barikongjoo myth in Korean Shamanism
    (2) The epic of Barikongjoo
    (3) The original *han* of Barikongjoo

(4) A symbolic interpretation of Bari's journey
  A. Father complex
  B. Mother complex
  C. Shadow
  D. Animus
  E. Persona
  F. The Self
  G. Vocation
2. The rituals of Korean Shamanism and *han*
  (1) The basic structure of Korean shaman rituals
  A. Chung-shin (invocation)
  B. Oh-shin (entertaining the gods)
  C. Song-shin (bidding the gods farewell)
  (2) Symbolism of the initiation ritual and *han*
  A. Huten kut (false gods ritual)
  B. Naerim kut (initiation ritual)
  C. Sosle kut (emergence ritual)

Chapter VI. The *han* in Korean Minjung Theology/135
1. Minjung Theology and *han*
2. The interpretation of *han* in Minjung Theology
  (1) *Han*, the feelings
  (2) *Han*, the suppressed and repressed feelings
  (3) *Han*, the subjective vs. the objective experience
  (4) The positive vs. negative aspects of *han*
  (5) A political interpretation of *han*
  (6) The internal vs. external origin of *han*
  (7) *Han* and "dan"
3. Toward a theology of healing

Chapter VII. Conclusion/163

Notes/167

Bibliography/185

CHAPTER I

INTRODUCTION

Deep within the unconscious mind lies the seedbed of human emotion--love, hate, regret, joy, sadness, greed, envy, etc.. The Korean soul has its own unique aspect, and in the Korean language it is called *han* (pronounced as hahn). The purpose of this study is to explore the root of *han* and to contribute to Minjung Theology in its understanding of *han*. The exploration of the root of *han* is a significant task on both the personal and collective levels. On the personal level, it may bring light into the darkest area of Korean minds, in which lies the source of both their suffering and creativity, pathology and health. On the collective level, it may equip them better in dealing with social contradictions and evils, by enhancing their capacity to discern and to find better solutions to them. The exploration of the root of *han* may provide Minjung Theology, a Christian theology grown in the soil of *han*, an opportunity to promote its self-understanding, as well as a needed substructure for its concept of *han*.

In the cultural tradition of Korea *han* has been generally acknowledged as the main source of creative activity in the realm of culture and religion. The themes of art--music, dance, and painting, as well as those of literature in its various forms (poetry, folktales, myths,

1

legends, novels, and theater)--are clustered around the *han*. Korean Shamanism, the indigenous religion that has served as the matrix of Korean culture throughout its history, has been developed around the reality of *han*. The shamans, the living symbol of han in Korea, become themselves through the experience of *han*, while the main pursuit of their rituals is to resolve the *han* of the people.

Han is a factor determining the quality of people's feelings and moods as experienced in their everyday life. As such, it is held responsible for emotional, psychosomatic, and mental disturbances that cause difficulties in interpersonal relationships. *Han* is most of all a psychological reality, formed through subjective experiences of the Korean people. Any discussion of an abstract idea of *han* can only add confusion to understanding it.

There are similar concepts in other Asian countries as well. In ancient India, for example, the Sanskrit "Upanaha" that originally had signified "fixation to things," developed into a more complex concept, encompassing hate, commotion, and evil emotion. In India, "Upanaha" is being used as the concept opposite to that of "Upanishad," which means living together. The Chinese word "Hen" means extreme grudge, revenge, hate, and curse, while the Mongolian word "Horosul" and the Manchurian word "Krosocuka" signify regret, sorrow, and depression.[1] In Japan, "Oorami" corresponds to the Korean *han*, as it relates to a wish by the spirit of the deceased to take revenge upon the living.[2]

The uniqueness of the Korean *han* lies in the richness of its meaning and in its relation to the everyday life of the people and their culture. Some elements of *han* can be seen in many other cultures, but when these elements are condensed into one reality *han* constitutes a unique Korean concept. And it is not identical to any of the similar concepts found in neighboring countries.[3]

Han is not a single feeling but many feelings condensed together, including resentment, regret, resignation, aggression, anxiety, loneliness, longing, sorrow, and emptiness. It even encompasses contradictory feelings such as hate and love. In *han*, these feelings interact with each other dynamically to create a specific *han* feeling depending on real circumstances.

The feelings of *han* have both positive and negative functions. On the one hand, it can enrich the subject's emotional life by mixing and condensing various ingredients of feelings to create the most subtle and sophisticated sentiments and moods. On the other, it can endanger the subject's emotional life by intensifying a certain feeling to an almost unbearable degree. The intensification of feeling is related to its suppression. When these feelings are suppressed for a long period they turn inside and become the feelings of *han*. Where there is suppression of emotion, there is *han*.

Beneath the suppressed feelings exist psychological wounds, which result from the experience of frustration and psychological pain. These wounds are responsible for the suppression of certain feelings, and thus for the creation of the *han* feelings. One crucial task of this study is to explore the inner wounds behind the feelings of *han* as deeply as possible. Beneath the secondary wounds accumulated throughout life exist the original wounds, formed during the period of early childhood. The original wounds are inevitable, because no one can pass the early childhood without experiencing frustration, fear, and psychological pain. They are like the original sin given to a person long before he can understand what it is, and how and why it originated. We are called upon to struggle with these original wounds and to heal them in the process of the maturation of the personality.

The original wounds, yet, do not primarily refer to the existential human nature, but to the psychological trauma that occurs in the earliest phase of the process of personality development. The degree of the wounds and of their healing varies. Some can be healed from their deep Does this mean, then, that all Koreans have their original wounds? The answer is yes. All Koreans have their wounds, just as all human beings have wounds, an inevitable fact of human life. This does not mean that all Koreans have pathology. Only those whose wounds that are deep and unhealed have the pathology of *han*. The uniqueness of *han* as a collective emotion of the Korean people lies in its relation to Korean culture and history. The reality of *han* has been acknowledged and treated as the central part of life and sublimated into a valuable human experience in their cultural and religious lives.

This does not mean that the reality of *han* has become obvious to Koreans. To assume that Koreans understand the full meaning of *han* simply by being Korean is a misconception. *Han* is an unknown, mysterious reality to Koreans themselves. They recognize that they share the cultural emotion of *han*, but the recognition of it is different from understanding it. It is yet another matter to understand it deeply and comprehensively. The understanding of *han* in its full nature is a needed and most challenging task.

The *han* expressed in the Korean indigenous religion--Korean Shamanism is rooted in an area of the mind deeper than the personal realm. This deeper aspect of *han* is a phenomenon related to what Carl G. Jung conceptualizes as collective unconscious. He discovered the existence of definite forms in the psyche that seem present always and everywhere. Mythological research calls them "motifs"; in the psychology of primitives they correspond to Levy-Bruhl's concept of "representations collectives"; and in the field of comparative religion they have been defined by Hubert and Mauss as "categories of imagination."[4] This deeper area of the mind may be called the cultural collective unconscious. Jung's concept, the collective unconscious, which is thought to be transcultural (as far as it transcends the diversity of cultural expressions), is compatible with the concept of the cultural collective unconscious. It recognizes common themes among the different cultures without violating the uniqueness of their individual cultural expressions. Yet, because the concept of the collective unconscious emphasizes the transcultural aspect, a new concept such as the cultural collective unconscious is needed to address the cultural aspect of the unconscious.

In Korean Shamanism, the shaman takes the role of mediator between the neither world and this world. She translates the private language of *han* into a language that can be understood by the people of a single culture. Through her mediating works, communication between the conscious and the unconscious, in psychological language, takes place. The language of *han*, as expressed in psychological symptoms of neurosis, borderline problems, and psychosis, is interpreted into the cultural symbolic language. This brings about reconciliation between the conscious and the unconscious, as well as between the personal and the collective unconscious.

In Korean culture, especially in Korean Shamanism, the psychological experience of *han* is transformed into a religious experience. It takes place when the voice of *han*, originating from the deeper layer of the mind (or, in Jung's language, from the objective psyche, which is synonymous with the collective unconscious), is heard and responded to by *han*-ridden people. According to Korean folk understanding, this listening to the voice of *han* brings forth the liberation of the soul from the bondage of *han*. This liberation can be understood as the psychological experience of transformation of personality and healing. This is why Korean Shamanism is viewed by most Korean scholars as a religious system. In Korean Shamanism the transformation of the psychological experience of *han* into a religious experience takes place.

The Korean Minjung Theology, which is rooted in the Korean experiences of life and culture, considers *han* to be the central theme of its theological enterprise. According to Nam-dong Suh, a major Minjung theologian, Minjung Theology is the theology of *han*. This study of *han*, therefore, is an effort to explore the core of Korean culture on the one hand and the root of Minjung Theology on the other. Despite its importance to Minjung Theology, the concept of *han* has not been thoroughly explored, and remains the most inexplicable part of Minjung Theology. The word *han* has been variously rendered by Minjung theologians as: a feeling of defeat, resignation, the tenacity of life, unresolved resentment, or grudge. These renderings, yet, can not fully convey the entire meaning of the reality of *han*. In this sense, Minjung theologians are right in deciding not to make any direct translation of the word *han* into other languages. However, this does not mean that the complexities of the concept need no further exploration and clarification. As a newly emerging world theology, Minjung Theology needs to continue its efforts to explore and define the experience of *han*. The efforts that have been made in the circle of Minjung Theology are concentrated on the socioeconomic dimension of *han*, in which *han* is identified with the subjective experience of those who have been oppressed politically, exploited economically, marginalized socially by the powerful and wealthy oppressors. *Han*, as a symbol for the cry of the oppressed people, has become a political metaphor in Minjung Theology in its struggle for social justice and political democracy. Yet *han* cannot be fully understood with the political interpretation only, because in deeper level it speaks to all people, oppressed and oppressor. The concept of *han* is the most mysterious and profound part of Minjung Theology both for Koreans and non-Koreans. As long as this concept remains vague on the grounds of its cultural exclusivity, it is impossible to bring Minjung Theology into a creative dialogue with other world theologies. Further, the *han* concept, which is so central to Minjung Theology, when left vague, inhibits communication and understanding. Although *han* is a Korean concept and symbol woven into and out of Korean history, it is a broad and deep image that speaks to all human beings about the mysterious source of both suffering and creativity. Therefore, in spite of the difficulties involved in explaining the concept of *han*, it should be translated into a language that promotes communication on a global level.[5]

The unique contribution to the understanding of *han*, which this study may bring about, is related to the use of depth psychology as the methodological tool. Because *han* is a psychological reality, existing in the deeper layer of the psyche, the most efficient tool for its exploration is depth psychology. Minjung Theology, which has used socioeconomic analysis as the main tool for the analysis of *han*, would also benefit from the use of depth psychology as a methodological tool. From the point of view of depth psychology, using especially the theories of Melanie Klein and of Carl G. Jung,[6] the inner nature of *han* and its meaning are interpreted. Their approaches to the psyche are significantly different; Klein stands in the tradition of psychoanalysis whereas Jung stands at the center of analytical psychology. Both approaches are needed in this study. Klein's theory can shed light on the area of the pathology of *han* and its inner dynamics. It is useful in sorting out the components of *han* and their interactions. But the psychoanalytic method, while it is indispensable for bringing some aspects of *han* into consciousness, cannot do justice to other of its aspects, such as the meaning of the psychic phenomena in relation to one's whole life. Certain meanings of *han* can be found only by making it whole, instead of fragmenting it. Thus synthesis is needed as well. Because *han* is not just the product of a certain cause, but also the carrier of a message from the unconscious, a synthetic method should be included. In the synthetic method focus was more on the meaning of the unconscious material as a whole than on the nature of each component of it, searching for the purpose and goal rather than the cause and origin. It treats the specific symbolic representations as having irreplaceable and irreducible values. It relates them to other phenomena based on similarities than distinguishing between them based on differences.[7] Carl G. Jung's approach to symbolism can be used to interpret the material of *han* produced by Korean culture in myths, fairy tales, and religious practices. With it *han* can be seen in a larger context of the whole life span. Especially in relation to the whole process of personality development or, in Jung's terms, "individuation process."

There are, of course, differences between the theories of Klein and Jung. The framework of their psychologies is different and may not be easily reconciled. This study doesn't reconcile these two theories but brings about an understanding of more facets of *han* reality. Though their premises are different, some of their basics are, in fact, compatible. Both emphasize the importance of the contents of fantasy, and both consider the negative aspect of the human psyche seriously. Klein finds the death instinct operating in the infant from birth, while Jung discovers the shadow, rooted in archetypal image of dark forces of evil. Klein's concept of death instinct seems related to the concept of original sin, whereas Jung's shadow is related to the original evil. Both concepts are related to the reality of *han*.[8]

The materials that are dealt with in this work come from published matter. These are records of history, poetry, essays, literary memos, myths, legends, fairy tales, descriptions of the rituals, and academic works in the field of Korean folklore, Shamanism, literature, and Minjung Theology.

The expressions of *han* of three individuals--King Yonsan, Sowol, and Eun Ko--are examined to explore the nature of *han* rooted in personality. These are chosen because their experiences of *han* are well known among Korean people. Both King Yonsan and Sowol have become symbolic figures of *han* in Korean history. Eun Ko is a person widely known in Korean society for his published materials of personal *han*. For King Yonsan's case, there are historical records written by the royal historians and private observers. For Sowol's *han*, his poems are considered as psychic materials of *han*. For Eun Ko's *han*, his diary memos, autobiography, dreams, and essays are available.

These individuals are all men, but the *han* of women is also an important part of this study. The *han* of women is focused on in chapter V, where the *han* in Korean Shamanism is discussed. Because shamans' *han* can be viewed as mainly feminine *han*. Besides, the expression of *han* in myth, legend, fairy tale, and ritual contains mainly the *han* of women. The three stories of "Barikongjoo," "Kongjui-Patjui," and "Emille Bell," which are important part of *han* material included in this study, have heroines.

In chapter II, the discoveries of the recent studies of *han* by Korean scholars from four different academic disciplines will be reviewed. These are the studies of folklore, Shamanism, literature, and psychology. This is to clarify the present status of the study of *han* and provide information on the proper direction for further study.

In chapter III, Melanie Klein's theories of the deepest area of the mind and their relationship to the concept of *han* will be discussed. With her two position theory the inner dynamics of the two prototypes of *han*--"wonhan" and "jeong-han"--will be examined. In addition, the third type of *han*--"huhan"--will be differentiated and conceptualized as a new category of *han*.

After establishing a theoretical basis by introducing the theories of Melanie Klein, in chapter IV the personal *han* of three individuals will be explored in light of her theories. It is illuminating to view King Yonsan from the Yi dynasty as representing "wonhan" (persecutory *han*); Sowol Kim from the period of Japanese rule as representing "jeong-han" (depressive *han*); and Eun Ko from modern times as representing "huhan" (schizoid *han*). It is true that not enough information about their lives exists to make a definitive analysis of them in terms of Melanie Klein's theory. Nonetheless, because the goal here is not defining personalities so much as exploring different levels of *han*, the available materials can be analyzed by that psychological theories suggestively, to point out aspects of *han*.

Korean Shamanism, the living tradition of Korean people's *han*, is dealt with in chapter V. The theories of Carl G. Jung are used as a guide in the interpretation of the shaman myths and rituals. Because of the vastness of material, only a few selected sources will be examined in this study. The "Barikongjoo" myth has been selected from among the myths of Korean Shamanism. The ritual of "naerim-kut" (initiation ritual) has been selected from among the rituals of Korean Shamanism. These two are chosen because they are the central myth and ritual, expressing the *han* of shamans themselves. The psychological interpretation of these myths and rituals will serve to reveal the basic dynamics involved in the Korean Shamanism--the transformation of personality.

The interpretation of *han* contained in the Korean Shamanism may add a new dimension to the world tradition of spirituality. For it provides insights and wisdom in dealing with evil forces that await us on our spiritual journey. In shaman ritual, a new spiritual realm, with its God or gods and evil spirits--a realm which Carl G. Jung called the world of archetypes--is opened.

In chapter VI, the works of five pioneers in the study of *han* in Minjung Theology will be discussed in relation to the depth psychological insights. These are the works of Nam-dong Suh, Young-hak Hyun, Dong-hwan Moon, Kwang-sun Suh, and Byung-mu Ahn. These theologians acknowledge the contribution of Chi-ha Kim and use him as an original source of reference. Accordingly, Chi-ha Kim's contribution to the understanding of *han* will be examined as an important part of Minjung Theology.

In chapter VII, based on the findings of the research, a few concluding remarks will be made on the nature of *han* in relation both to the understanding of *han* in Korean culture and in Korean Minjung Theology.

CHAPTER II

A REVIEW OF THE RECENT STUDIES OF *HAN*

Since the 1970's, there have been many discussions on the subject of *han* in the fields of folklore, Shamanism, literature, psychology and theology. Except for the theories developed in the theological field, which will be dealt with separately in chapter VI, this chapter will examine the existing theories and discoveries on the subject of *han* produced in the other four branches of Korean academy.

1. Folklore Study

(1) The Repressed Sexual Libido

Kyu-tae Lee discovers *han* in the stories of Korean legends and myths. Using Freud's concept of libido, he interprets *han* as repressed libido. When sexual libido cannot find expression, due to moral and social inhibition, it becomes *han*. His interpretation is also based on the folklore understanding of *han*, as expressed in Korean legends and myths. In the myriad of stories of *han*, young men or women became "mongdang-guishin" (bachelor-ghosts) or "songaksi" (maiden-ghosts) because they had died before having a chance to discharge their sexual libido. He finds the prototype of *han* in these figures.[1]

Although Lee does not mention the relationship between *han* and Freud's early theory of anxiety, his interpretation of *han* is closely related to libido theory; the sexual libido, which is rejected or not used by ego, gets discharged as anxiety.[2]

Lee's interpretation however, is limited by equating *han* with only sexual instinct. He does not consider that in human beings there are instincts other than the sexual. For example, the instinct for self realization, which is a more fundamental than sexual instinct for Jung,[3] or the instinct for meaning, for Victor Frankl.[4] Despite its limitations, yet, this interpretation contributes to the understanding of *han* by bringing light to the sexual aspect of it.

(2) The Korean Complex

Relating *han* to the Jungian concept of the complex, Yul-kyu Kim understands *han* as a psychological complex of the Korean people. By the word "complex" he means, a psychological entity existing in the Korean psyche and exerting its influence upon the lives of Korean people.[5] According to him, *han* originates in and is nurtured by death, especially death in distress.[6] It grabs people sadistically or masochistically through the power of the unconscious.[7] Using the mechanism of projection, which is the most visible characteristic of its inner nature, *han* blames and seeks revenge upon others, thereby producing innocent victims. Because it imputes woe to others indiscriminately, it can be properly called paranoid.[8] *Han* calls for revenge, which in turn calls for further revenge; it is a vicious circle ever increasing its intensity. Kim calls this negative aspect "the dark transference of *han*." He also notices the positive aspect of *han* that can be sublimated into an achievement motive through self decision. It may become the basis for a consciousness of ethics when it does break off the vicious circle of impersonal forces. This positive aspect he calls "the bright transference of *han*."[9]

Yul-kyu Kim also confirms that *han* is not only a personal complex but also a collective complex of the Korean people inherited from past generations. It is the product of social and cultural conditions throughout Korean history. These are repeated foreign invasions, political oppression by powerful elite, and interpersonal conflicts among family members in the large family system.[10]

Collective *han* generates power to change history, for good or bad. When it becomes collective, individual vengeance transforms into public anger, which is the source of energy for the achievement of social justice or injustice. In this way it may serve the will of Heaven,[11] or defy it. In Korean history the "Tonghak Revolution"[12] can be counted as an example of the positive expression of collective *han*.[13] In that revolution the bright transference of *han* took place, since the revolution contributed to the enhancement to the humanity of the Korean people. On the other hand, there are also examples of collective negative *han*, which is much more destructive than individual negative *han*. The vicious circle of political party strife, which troubled the entire population of the country throughout the five hundred year history of the Yi dynasty, is a good example of the dark transference of collective *han*. Although Kim's research on *han* provides many insights into its nature, he does not explain how these attributes are interrelated. Remaining unanswered are such questions as: How is *han* originated in and nurtured by death? How is it related to sadism and masochism? What are the inner relationships between the bright transference of *han* and the dark transference of it?

Despite the limitations Kim's study is significant, because it articulates the Korean folk understanding of *han*. Thus, in this study his findings are used as a reference to Korean cultural understanding of *han*. One important aspect of his contribution to the understanding of *han* is that he relates *han* to the psychic reality, existing in a deeper area of psyche than the ordinary consciousness of the Korean people.

2. Korean Shamanism

Until recently, most of the studies of Korean Shamanism have focused on the phenomenological description of shaman rituals and practices. Interpretations of the symbolism of Shamanism are very scarce, but there are a few significant studies that suggest the centrality of *han* in Korean Shamanism. In these studies, *han* is considerd the key concept in explaining the phenomenon of "sinbyung" (shaman sickness).

(1) Deep Wounds

Young-sook Kim Harvey considers "sinbyung" to be the central concept for understanding Korean Shamanism in which "sinbyung" is believed to be the bodily expression of *han*. "Sinbyung" literally means sickness brought on by spirits, and it refers to a range of somatic, mental, and behavioral symptoms. Through the processes of suffering and healing the "sinbyung" shamans are born. She views "sinbyung" as the result of the severe conflicts between the shamans' self-image and cultural definition of them from their childhood period.[14] She finds at the bottom of these conflicts "a deep and abiding sense of having been morally injured as human beings."[15] For her, *han* is a deep, abiding psychological wound that brings about the "sinbyung."

(2) Frustrated Wish for Eternity

Tae-gon Kim approaches the "sinbyung" phenomenon from the perspective of the psychology of religion. To him, *han* is a frustrated wish for the eternal in the face of one's finitude of being, which expresses itself in the symptom of "sinbyung." "Sinbyung" is primarily a psychological phenomenon. Yet because of the cultural and religious environment of Shamanism, it is experienced as a religious phenomenon and understood as a religious sickness.[16] Psychologically, "sinbyung" is a dissociation of consciousness that is spurred by the traumatic experience of everyday life. Because of the dissociation of consciousness, the archetypal religiosity that had been hidden in the unconscious is exposed. The exposed archetypal unconscious material is perceived and understood in the belief system of Korean Shamanism as a religious phenomenon. When the same phenomenon takes place and is understood in a different religious environment, for example, in Christianity, it is perceived as the so called "experience of the Holy Spirit."[17]

For Tae-gon Kim, whose research on Shamanism is guided by the works of Mircea Eliade, *han* consists of traumatic experiences from everyday life. The essence of these traumatic experiences is a frustrated wish for the eternal in the face of one's finitude of being. He views that human beings are existentially vulnerable, as they are constantly exposed to these experiences that may cause the dissociation of the consciousness. When one comes to the realization that one is a finite being, one's wish for eternity becomes *han* out of despair. This is how *han* is created in people. And when one's *han* is serious, it expresses itself in "sinbyung," a dissociation of the consciousness. This breakdown easily takes place when people experience the death of someone with whom they are closely associated. Thus *han* is an inevitable, existential, human problem whose origin lies in the religious wish for eternity. This wish flows out of the archetypal layer of the unconscious, expressed through shamanistic phenomena.[18] Yet Kim does not explain why only some people experience "sinbyung" if, as he views it, *han* is an existential phenomenon that results from the frustrated wish for eternity.

3. Korean Literature: "Jeong-han" vs. "Wonhan"

Han has been a traditional theme of Korean literature, from the oldest poem to the modern forms of literature.[19] Hun-young Im summarizes the discussions about *han* in the Korean literary tradition in two large streams: *han* as an individual, sentimental, lyric, pessimistic, and regressive emotion; and *han* as the emotion of anger that is the energy for social and historical change. The former, "jeong-han" sets off a chain reaction of resignation, adaptation to reality, and national nihilism, whereas the latter, "wonhan" results in vengeance, social conscientization, and revolution.[20]

Traditionally "jeong-han" has been the proper theme of literature, but a new trend, emphasizing "wonhan" and its function, is arising to challenge the old tradition. This challenge is most apparent in Eun Ko's assertion that "wonhan" is the authentic national emotion of *han* than "jeong-han," which is the secondary national emotion. For him, "jeong-han," a feminine *han*, is a corrupted form of the original masculine "wonhan" and is the result of repeated historical experiences of being defeated, subjugated, and humiliated. He advocates the recovery of the masculine *han*, the "wonhan."[21]

Hun-young Im, on the other hand, acknowledging the intrinsic value of both streams of *han*, tries to reconcile them. He suggests that revolution should not be imposed upon the "*minjung*" (people who are poor and powerless). He believes the will for social change can be created through the creation of community and culture, which can be achieved through resolving the individual *han* in the group. In the practice of Korean Shamanism, for example, the primary goal is to resolve the individual *han*, during which a transformation of the consciousness takes place. Individualistic concerns are enlarged to become social and communal concerns. Thus, both streams of *han* can contribute to personal as well as social change. Both elements of *han*--"jeong" (love) and "won" (aggression)--are needed to bring about its resolution.[22]

A clear cut distinction between "jeong-han" and "wonhan" is impossible to make, because in reality they exist in a mixture of the two. When the element of "jeong" is stronger, it becomes "jeong-han," whereas when the element of "won" is stronger, it becomes "wonhan." Despite all the possible fluctuations between "jeong" and "won," there are certain patterns in an individual's *han* that tend to move toward love or aggression. They coexist but sometimes conflict each other. Thus Hun-young Im understands the history of Korean literature as the history of the confrontation between "jeong-han" and "wonhan."[23]

4. Psychological Studies

In the studies of psychoanalysis and analytical psychology, the problem of *han* is delved into by two pioneers; Bou-yong Rhie and Kwang-il Kim.

(1) Unlived Life

In his article, "Illness and Healing in the Three Kingdom Period: A Symbolical Interpretation," Bou-yong Rhie points out that in Korean traditional belief *han* is considered the primary cause of disease. "The grudge of the living and the dead was an object of fear not only for the kings during the Three Kingdom Period but also the kings of 'Koryu' and the 'Chosen dynasty' (Yi dynasty) who held offering ceremonies for the spirits of the dead to console them, whenever epidemic disease broke out." Here Rhie renders *han* as "grudge."[24] In another article, "Dealing with Evil in Korean Fairy Tales," Rhie also points out that *han* is the soil where evil grows. The soul of a person who died in an unhappy state plays an important role in folk tales of evil.[25] According to Korean folk belief, *han* is the soul of a person who died in an unhappy state. In this tradition, *han* is projected onto the dead. The "grudge" of the dead, however, as interpreted by Rhie, is in reality the grudge of the living. Because the grudge results from the unlived life, the essence of *han* can be understood as the grudge that results from an "unlived life."

> When you really live with your self, you need not bear a grudge after death. But, when you are dependent on the collective codex, keeping your face, and never living your life sufficiently, there remains an unlived life which is projected onto the idea of the grudge of the soul.[26]

(2) Negative Mother Complex

Evil is the personification of *han*. In Korean folk tales, evil appears to people to ask for the resolution of the grudge of the dead. When the "grudge," or the *han*, is resolved, the evil disappears.[27] In Korean folk tales almost all evils can be driven away or killed. There are some rare stories in which no effort is made by the hero to fight against evil, nor is there any successful escape from evil, let alone the conquering of it. Bou-yong Rhie provides an example of a story of absolute evil and its psychological meaning.

> Once upon a time a mother and her son were living together. Everyday the son went to the mountain and the mother always prepared lunch for him--some cooked rice and a little Kochujang (Korean bean and pepper puree). One day, the son asked her to give him more Kochujang for his lunch, and she did so. At noon, in the forest, he finished his lunch, but a little Kochujang remained. He wished to use it all. A skull rolled toward him, so he smeared the Kochujang on the skull

and was about to leave the place. At that moment, the skull began to talk to him: 'Come with me!' He followed the skull. The skull disappeared, and a big traditional Korean house with a tiled roof before him. It began to rain hard, so he had no choice but to enter into the house. A white haired old woman said well to him, 'Oh, you are coming now. I waited for you for a long time. I was sure you would come.' She cooked rice and brought it to him with Kochujang. He ate the meal. The old woman asked him to tell her a fairy tale. He wouldn't. But, upon her repeated request, he told her what had happened to him just before. The old woman nodded and murmured; 'Ah, so?,' and all of a sudden she threw a somersault three times. She then became a fox and ate the man.[28]

In this story there is no struggle with evil, as the victim is helpless and behaves passively toward evil. The beloved food of Korea, Kochujang, plays an important role in the story, representing an object that has an animating power. Thus, by smearing the skull with Kochujang it could come alive and able to talk. The red color of Kochujang has a meaning as well, as it is a color that is supposed to have the power to drive away evil in Siberian Shamanism. Psychologically, the red color indicates temperament and passion, which can be identified as warm affect. The man in the story demands too much affection from his mother. And the old woman in the forest who behaves like the man's own mother (offering him cooked rice and Kochujang) has certain ties with the man's mother at home.

Accordingly, the story tells about the danger of a negative mother complex. The young man demands more Kochujang. This means, the man demands more affection from his mother. With this excessive affection he stimulates the deep-seated maternal instinct of his unconscious, which had remained untouched in his mind like the skull in this tale and waited a long time to be consciously expressed.[29] The young man represents the ego of our total psyche, while the old woman is a representation of the negative mother archetype. The old woman changed into a fox and ate the man, meaning that the ego was overwhelmed and entirely possessed by the archetypal maternal instinct.

The consequence is a psychotic breakdown in which the ego function is absolutely controlled by the power of mythical components.[30]

According to Bou-yong Rhie's psychological interpretation of Korean fairy tales, the deep seat of *han* (as the source of evil) is in the "negative mother complex."[31] He relates the negative mother complex directly to the function of archetype in the collective unconscious, without explaining the cause of the formation of the negative mother complex in an individual.

This story and others illustrate that there are cases in which it is better not to provoke the unconscious by the stimulation of fantasies and dreams, because it may result in a psychotic breakdown.[32] The wisdom contained in these stories is that if the *han* is deep and extreme, caution and tenderness, not confrontation, should be used to deal with it. This wisdom is also found in the practice of Korean Shamanism in which, while some evils can be expelled by the power of good spirits, certain evils may only be appeased by offering food and entertainment.[33] The psychological meaning of these stories of allegedly unbeatable evil is related to the nature of *han*. If the *han* is extremely severe, then it should be treated with the utmost care to avoid a psychotic breakdown.

(3) Split-off Part of Ego

In the article "The Relationship Between Death and *Han*," Bou-yong Rhie clarifies the relationship between death and *han*. Here he views *han* as a split-off part of the ego that results from the sudden experience of the death of a person with whom one is identified. The death of a closely related person always entails a forfeit of a portion of the consciousness of the bereaved. The degree of the subjective loss depends upon the degree of the identification. The split-off part of the ego remains in the unconscious and forms a powerful complex, which is called *han*.[34]

In summary, Bou-yong Rhie's concept of *han* consists of three components: the grudge of an unlived life, the negative mother complex, and the split-off ego. *Han* is the grudge of an unlived life in a general sense. When serious, it finds its source in a negative mother complex. It is also a complex incorporating the split ego because of the experience of the death of the loved person. Rhie acknowledges the existence of a layer of *han* that is formed by unexpressed libido. This idea of *han* is related to Kyu-tae Lee's understanding of *han* as repressed sexual libido. The difference between them is that Bou-yong Rhie understands libido as the energy for both sexual and spiritual life, whereas Kyu-tae Lee understands libido as solely sexual energy. Furthermore, for Bou-yong Rhie *han* has more dimensions than just unlived libido. In its more serious forms, it is related to the negative mother complex and to the split of the ego. Here arise a few questions: Why do some people not live their lives fully and thus create *han*, whereas others can sufficiently enjoy their lives and die without leaving *han*? Why do some people develop a negative mother complex and become carriers of serious *han*? The death of the loved person is a universal human experience, without exception; Why, then, are some people unable to withstand this common human tragedy and suffer a psychological breakdown?

It seems that when one experiences the loss of a loved one, one experiences not only the loss of the part of the ego but also the reactivation of the original fragmentation of the ego, existing in a deep layer of one's personal unconscious. The current experience of loss stimulates and reactivates the deep seated original wounds (or original *han*), formed during the early days of life. If one has a healthy ego without excessive original wounds, one is able to enjoy life sufficiently and endure big or small losses during one's life. On the other hand, if one has a weak or an immature ego due to serious original wounds formed during the early days of life, the experience of loss is liable to cause one to reexperience the original loss in addition to the current loss. In an attempt to avoid the danger of exposing the original wounds, one represses one's own feelings and ideas, and thus the libido itself.

In the psychological paradigm of Bou-yong Rhie, the deeper original wounds are equivalent to the negative mother complex, though he doesn't provide an explicit explanation for it. He attributes the formation of the negative mother complex to the influence of the mother archetype, which is a collective, universal, and mythical phenomenon than an individual, personal, and historical one. By doing so, he leaves the personal side of the negative mother complex unexplained.

(4) Split Infantile Mother Imago

The personal side of the negative mother complex is explored by Kwang-il Kim in his psychoanalytic study of "sinbyung." He contributes to the understanding of *han* through his psychoanalytic study of Korean Shamanism. His clinical study of "sinbyung" provides indispensable insights into the inner dynamics of *han*, as "sinbyung" is essentially the expression of *han*. "Sinbyung" is primarily a symptom of psychic disturbance. This view is accepted by most Korean scholars.[35] In his article, "Psychoanalysis of Sinbyung," Kim explicates the psychodynamics of four cases of "sinbyung." The four individuals involved were treated by him in a psychiatric ward setting between 1966 to 1969, during which time the contents of their unconscious fantasies were thoroughly analyzed. They were under the influence of the world view of Korean Shamanism and had symptoms identical with those of "sinbyung." They were diagnosed as having "sinbyung" by their "mutangs" (shamans) during the "kut" (shaman ritual), who they sought out before seeking psychiatric care. The four happened to be women, and this indicates that "sinbyung" is more closely associated with the *han* of women than of men. The following report is an excerpt from the clinical records of the four cases of "sinbyung."[36]

A. Case 1. Female, 32 years old.

She recalls her mother as a cold woman who ignored her at home. The recurring theme in her dreams is centered on the persecutory image of her mother. In one dream, a woman threw her in a fire, and the people around her told her that she was her mother. In another, a shaman tried to kill her with evil spirits, and her mother, wearing shaman's clothing, cursed her and threatened to kill her with a knife. She is afraid of the shaman but also feels she has to become a shaman.[37]

Kim points out that the persecutory image of shaman in her dream is the infantile image of her mother that has been transferred to the image of a shaman. Her unconscious is trying to cope with the persecutory fear of her mother by projecting it onto the shaman. Thus she is trying to overcome the fear by identifying herself with the persecutor, the shaman.[38]

B. Case 2. Female, 30 years old.

She recalls her mother as a person who constantly nags and treats her unfairly as compared to her brother. She hates and fears her mother and her mother-in-law. When her mother-in-law is absent from home, her psychotic symptoms clear up; with her return the symptoms reappear. She feels comfortable at the shaman's home. During the shaman ritual she feels so happy that she dances and sings with a loud voice.[39]

Kim finds in this patient aggression toward the mother, but the aggression is not projected onto a shaman. On the contrary, she projects an ideal, loving mother image onto the shaman. The aggression toward her mother is projected onto her mother-in-law. In her unconscious, her mother is split in two: good and bad.[40]

C. Case 3. Female, 32 years old.

For six months she has been hearing women's voices inside her belly saying "You sinned against me and should be ashamed of yourself." When she went to see a shaman two years ago, the shaman told her that the spirits of her grandmother and her mother had intruded into her body. She hated her mother during her childhood, but since her death from illness when the subject was 13 years old, she has felt guilty about her hatred of her mother. She had suffered greatly under her stepmother's harsh and unfair treatment, so for her, the shaman is like a good mother who she can trust.[41]

Kim views the origin of the "sinbyung" of this woman in the split image of her mother. Her mother image is split in two parts: the ideal mother and the persecutory mother. The ideal mother is projected onto the "mutang," while the bad, persecutory mother is projected onto her mother and grandmother. The bad experience of her stepmother intensified the bad mother aspect. Her guilt toward her mother, which creates the unconscious feeling that she deserves punishment, intensifies the persecutory aspect of the bad mother as well. She is in a relationship of symbiotic dependence with her mother whose imago is split in two.[42]

D. Case 4. Female, 35 years old.

She believes that the spirit of her grandfather-in-law entered her body, and she hears his voice calling her. The immediate cause of her symptoms was her grandfather-in-law's suicide two years ago. She felt sadness and the futility of life upon his tragic death. Her mother divorced her father when the subject was three years old. She grew up under the care of her stepmother who she hated very much. She is afraid of the "mutang" as much as she is of her stepmother. She has hallucinations in which bad spirits try to kill her and eat her, and then the spirit of the grandfather-in-law fights with the bad spirits and chases them away. She hates to become a "mutang" herself, but she feels that if she does, the bad spirits would obey her.[43]

Kwang-il Kim finds again in these cases that the parental image of the patient's early childhood is the cause of the "sinbyung." Oedipal aggression operates in the patient's relationship to her mother. The triangular relationship between the patient, the good grandfather spirit, and the "mutang" (or the bad spirits) is a reactivation of the Oedipal relationship between the patient and her mother and father. To cope with the pain arising from the Oedipal conflict, she identifies with the aggressor and considers becoming a "mutang."[44]

Based on the analysis of the above four cases of "sinbyung," Kwang-il Kim makes three concluding remarks. First, "sinbyung" is a psychological phenomenon that takes place when the ego breaks down due to its inability to cope with the pain of reality. Then a secondary personality, existing in the unconscious, is reactivated and projected onto the cultural system of Shamanism and recognized as "sinbyung." Second, "sinbyung" is the cultural expression of inner aggression that has been repressed in and suppressed by the society. Third, "sinbyung" is a way of achieving an infantile fantasy that was rejected in reality. In "sinbyung" there is a regression to the infantile psychology from which the aggression toward the parents arises.[45]

Kim suggests that the psychological dynamics of "sinbyung" are not very different from those of mental illnesses such as paranoid schizophrenia, hysteria, or psycho-somatic disturbance. These three conditions may overlap, or a subject may move from one to another.[46]

When the *han* is projected onto Shamanism, it gets cultural meaning and can be managed, healed, and transformed into a useful source for the service of the community. The person who suffered "sinbyung" becomes a shaman to heal the *han* of other people in the society. With his psychoanalysis of "sinbyung," Kwang-il Kim provides some insights into the nature of *han*. He illustrates the existence of "the secondary personality"[47] that reveals itself after the breakdown of the conscious ego. This secondary personality is equivalent to the original wounds (or the original *han*) whose basic psychological elements are aggression, persecutory fear, and a split-off image of the mother.

Kwang-il Kim approaches the negative mother complex from the perspective of the personal, psychological experience of a child in relation to its mother, whereas Bou-yong Rhie approaches it from the perspective of collective archetypal images. Both studies provide a foundation for the further psychological study of *han*.

5. The Original and the Secondary *Han*.

From the examination of the existing theoretical concepts of *han* in the four disciplines of study: folklore, shamanism, literature, and psychology, it can be concluded that there exists a layer of an original type of *han*. For Yul-kyu Kim, *han* is a complex hidden deep in people's minds. It erupts uncontrollably to tear ourselves apart and to harm others, destroying interpersonal relationships. It is inherited through the generations and thus became an archetypal psychic reality of the Korean people.[48] For Kim, *han* is something different from the consequences of the experiences of everyday life. It is something original, distinguished from the secondary *han* that is accumulated in everyday life as certain memories, which can be recalled with or without effort.

Both Young-sook Kim Harvey and Tae-gon Kim confirm the existence of an original *han* in their studies of the shamans who are *han*-ridden people. Young-sook Kim Harvey finds a deep sense of moral injury to be the cause of "sinbyung." Tae-gon Kim finds the ultimate cause of "sinbyung" in the gap between religious instinct and reality that results in a personal psychological wound. This wound is exposed when a dissociation of the conscious ego occurs by the experiences of frustration in everyday life. Without making it explicit, both authors imply in their discussions an original type of psychological wounds that is distinguished from the ordinary psychological wounds that may result from everyday life experiences.

In the tradition of Korean literature, the positions of "jeong-han" and ""wonhan" are well established. Given all the variations and fluctuations between the two emotions, they serve as the two prototypes of *han*. The concept of original *han* is congruent with the literary tradition that behind the innumerable phenomena of *han* exist the two original types, "wonhan" and "jeong-han."

Analytical psychology and psychoanalysis complement one another in the study of *han*. Bou-yong Rhie, who represents analytical psychology, finds the negative mother complex to be the seedbed of *han*. By relating its origin to this archetypal psychic reality, he posits the reality of *han* in a deeper layer of the collective unconscious. For him, this type of *han* is something original and is the primary cause of the ordinary experience of the unfulfilled wish or undischarged emotions. Kwang-il Kim, who stands in the psychoanalytic tradition, also probes the area of the mind that is formed through one's relation to one's mother in early childhood. In his study of the cases of "sinbyung," Kim clarifies that the cause of the dissociation of the ego lies in the original *han*, which he calls the "secondary personality." The immediate cause of the dissociation of the ego is, of course, a certain traumatic experience in one's current life that is strong enough to dissociate consciousness. A single isolated experience of great suffering may bring forth the breakdown of the ego, but usually this seemingly isolated experience has some connection to past experiences of *han*, especially a childhood traumatic experience.

Beneath the layer of *han* that is accumulated throughout the course of life starting with the late childhood period, exists another, more primordial part, which can be called the original *han*. Original *han* is beyond the reach of conscious memory, since it is formed during the early days of childhood. Though the original *han* remains in the personal unconsciousness and is unavailable to conscious memory, it still exerts great influence upon one's moods and conscious thought processes. It intensifies and exaggerates the proportions of the current experience of suffering by reactivating primitive anxiety to the extent that the current experience of *han* becomes nearly unbearable.

It may be assumed that original *han* defies an easy integration into the total personality and tends to remain an alien part of the self in one's personality. Yet, it is not content to remain in silence, for it consists essentially of the life energy that is repressed without having the chance to express itself. It strives constantly to express itself through feelings, dream images, various psycho-somatic symptoms, or through compulsive "acting outs."

The ego, using its defense mechanisms, tries to force the original *han* to remain in the unconscious. The ego represses feelings and ideas arising from the unconscious because they contain the material of the original *han* that is felt as overwhelming pain and, as such, is a threat to the ego. The life energy is repressed, which adds more material for *han*. In this way the *han* as the "grudge of unlived life" is produced as a general part of *han*.

Over the course of the years, many experiences of suffering may be accumulated around the original *han*, and the original *han* may remain unmodified by the secondary *han*. Only when the original *han* is healed, modified, or sublimated, can the secondary *han* be sustained, overcome, and creatively sublimated. Therefore, dealing with the secondary *han* is not enough. The deeper part of *han* must be penetrated and healed to bring a change in one's personality.

CHAPTER III

THE INNER DYNAMICS OF THE ORIGINAL *HAN*

In the previous chapter the concept of the original *han* could be derived from the existing interpretations of *han* in Korea. Because the original *han* is formed through the early experiences of childhood in relation to parents, especially mother, it is necessary to explore the inner dynamics of the early childhood experiences in order to understand the nature of the original *han*. For this purpose the psychological findings of Melanie Klein can be used as theoretical tools to penetrate the deep layer of the psyche.

1. Melanie Klein and Child Analysis

Melanie Klein was born in Vienna in 1882 as the youngest of the four children in a Jewish family, grew up in a liberal family atmosphere, married at the age of twenty-one, and had three children.[1] She found Freud through his works on psychoanalysis in Budapest in around 1910, became a pupil of Ferenczi and a follower of Freud. She was also influenced by Karl Abraham who gave her warm supports and encouragements. Throughout her life, which was devoted to the

27

advancement of psychoanalysis, until she died in London in 1960 at the age of 78, she made a great contribution to the knowledge of the deepest area of human mind.[2]

Freud was a pioneer in child analysis. In 1905 he published the case of Little Hans, a five year old boy. Under Freud's supervision his father analyzed him and uncovered his Oedipus complex.[3] Little effort was made for more than ten years until Melanie Klein started child analysis with a new technique: the play technique.[4]

Klein found that the child's natural mode of expressing itself was play. A child expresses its phantasies, its wishes and its actual experiences in a symbolic way through play and games.[5] Klein spells the word "phantasy" with a "ph" to emphasize the psychoanalytic meaning of the term, that is, that phantasy operates unconsciously, as opposed to "fantasy," which we consciously know about and engage in as daydreaming. The symbolism expressed in the child's play can be interpreted in the same way the adult's dream material is interpreted. The archaic and symbolic forms of representation that the child employs in its play are associated with another primitive mechanism, "acting out." The "acting out" in child's play contains the contents of the child's unconscious. Play is the major route of access to the child's unconscious.

As the content of the play phantasy is important, because "all impulses, all feelings, all modes of defense are experienced in phantasy, which gives them mental life and shows their direction and purpose."[6] The understanding of phantasy world provides insights into the inner world of *han*, for it is filled with phantasies.

In her paper on "The Technique of Early Analysis" Klein provides the cases of the analyses of little children to illustrate the symbolism of the child's play and her technique in analyzing it. Peter was a little child of three years and nine months when he came for his first session.

> He took two horse-drawn carriages and bumped one into another, so that the horses' feet knocked together, and said; "I've got a new little brother called Fritz." I asked him what the carriages were doing. He answered; "That's not nice," and stopped bumping them together at once, but started again quite

soon. Then he knocked two toy horses together in the same
way. Upon which I said; "Look here, the horses are two
people bumping together." At first he said; "No, That's not
nice," but then, "Yes, that's two people bumping together,"
and added; "The horses have bumped together too, and now
they're going to sleep." Then he covered them up with bricks
and said: "Now they're quite dead; I've buried them."[7]

In this session Klein only drew attention to the symbolic meaning of
the toys. As the session continues she could draw out the contents of his
unconscious wishes and phantasies. She could find in his symbolic play
his Oedipus conflicts and his conflicts around his bisexuality, and at
bottom his death wish to his parents and brother, which is already
indicated in this first session by his saying, "they're dead."

In the analysis of Erna, a little girl of six who suffered from a
severe obsessional neurosis, Klein revealed that the girl's phantasy was
colored with sadism, oral and anal. In her play she put a toy man and
a toy woman together and said they were to love one another. And soon
she made a third figure, a little man, who ran them over, killed and
roasted them, and then ate them up. In other games she was in her
phantasy soiling, burning, and poisoning the parental figures using her
feces and urine. These games reveal the oral and anal sadistic attacks on
her parents.

The analysis of Rita, age two and three-quarters years, a severely
disturbed child with night terrors, showed that such phantasies and fears
were already operating in a very small child. She was inhibited in play,
oversensitive to reproach, and overburdened with excessive guilt and
anxiety. In her phantasy her mother was a prohibiting persecutory figure
who was different from her real mother. When she played with a doll
she took no pleasure in it and kept saying that the doll was not her child.
Klein discovers an internalized object as the source of fear in this little
girl.

Analysis showed that she was not permitted to play at being its mother, because,
among other things, the doll child stood for her little brother who she had wanted
to steal from her mother during the latter's pregnancy. The prohibition,

however, did not proceed from her real mother, but from an introjected one who treated her with far more severity and cruelty than the real one had ever done.[8]

Ruth, a four year old girl, was one of those children whose ambivalence shows itself in an over-strong fixation upon the mother and certain other women, while they dislike others. Analysis revealed that she was suffering repeated anxiety attacks during her play, and a further analysis brought out that there was a repetition of night terror, from which she had suffered very severely at the age of two.

At that time her mother had been pregnant, and the little girl's wish to steal the new baby out of her mother's body and to hurt and kill her by various means had brought on a strong reaction against these wishes that manifested itself as a sense of guilt in the child, in consequence of which she had become unusually strongly fixated upon her mother. Saying good-night before she went to sleep meant saying goodbye for ever. Because of her desires to rob and kill her mother, she was afraid of being abandoned by her forever or of never seeing her alive again, or of finding, in the place of the kind and tender mother who was saying good-night to her, a "bad" mother who would attack her in the night.[9]

Klein paid attention to the intensity of the child's anxiety and child's need to use defense mechanisms against it. The child tries to protect itself against the anxiety produced by threatening internal figures by splitting them off and projecting them outside, and at the same time tries to introject idealized parental figures. Thus, by the processes of projection and introjection, the child gradually builds up an internal world of ideal and persecutory objects split off from one another, kept far apart. These mechanisms of splitting and projection are a principal factor in the tendency to personification in play.[10]

As Freud discovered the repressed child in the adult, Klein discovered the repressed infant in the child. She became increasingly convinced that children were dominated by their unconscious relation to the already repressed internal figures of the oral phase.[11]

The features of the repressed internal figures revealed in the analyses of the play and games of Peter, Erna, Rita, and Ruth are not much different from the internal nature of the four cases of "sinbyung" that were analyzed by Kwang-il Kim as described in chapter II. The common elements are persecutory fear, split image of parents (especially of mother) into good and bad, projection, identification, and aggression.

2. Melanie Klein's Theory of Anxiety

(1) Persecutory Anxiety

Based on the clinical evidence accumulated in the analyses of young children, Klein contends that the primary anxiety is the fear of annihilation. By connecting this fear of annihilation to Freud's theory of the death instinct, she suggests that the original source of anxiety is the death instinct, from which arises the fear of annihilation. For an illustration she provides the following case materials.

> A five-year-old boy used to pretend that he had all sorts of wild animals, such as elephants, leopards, hyenas and wolves, to help him against his enemies. They represented dangerous objects that he had tamed and could use as protection against his enemies. But it appeared in the analysis that they also stood for his own sadism, each animal representing a specific source of sadism. The elephants symbolized his muscular sadism, his impulses to trample and stamp. The tearing leopards represented his teeth and nails and their function in his attacks. The wolves symbolized his excrement invested with destructive properties. He sometimes became very frightened that the wild animals he had tamed would turn against him and exterminate him. The fear expressed his sense of being threatened by his own destructiveness (as well as by internal persecutors).[12]

In this child his sadism, which is represented as aggressive animals, is related to the fear of death. The fear of death comes from the death instinct that is the source for the sadism. Klein sees the death instinct as operating from birth, as does the life instinct. The death instinct is the ultimate source of primary anxiety, the fear of annihilation that the helpless infant experiences in face of internal and external dangers. The primary danger situation arising from the activity of the death instinct is felt by the child as persecution.[13]

Klein assumes that the struggle between the life and death instincts already operates during birth and accentuates the persecutory anxiety aroused by this painful experience. This experience has the effect of making the first external object, the mother's breast, appear hostile.[14] Thus the ego turns the destructive impulses against this primary object. Any frustration by the breast is felt by the infant as retaliation and persecution for his destructive impulses toward it. In these ways the breast becomes the bad breast. Then the bad breast is introjected and forms an internal bad object.

There is a constant vicious circle between the fear of internal and external bad objects, between the death instinct acting within and deflected outward. In this dynamic process the persecutory anxiety acquires more contents and increases its intensity. Also one's aggression toward the persecutory objects is intensified, for anxiety and aggression reinforce each other. At first the infant's aggressive impulse through projection plays an important role in building up persecutory figures, and then these very figures increase the persecutory anxiety and in turn reinforce the aggressive impulses. Because the infant's ego tries to defend itself by defeating the persecutory objects, when persecutory anxiety becomes stronger the aggression is also intensified.[15]

This process consists of two lines of chain reactions and the interaction between them. First, the struggle between life and death instincts, -- persecutory anxiety, -- aggression as the reaction to the anxiety, -- intensified persecutory anxiety. Second, the deflection of the death instinct, -- persecutory breast, -- experience of frustration, -- bad breast, -- introjected and then becomes the object of the fear, -- intensified persecutory anxiety.

Klein contends that every infant experiences persecutory anxiety as part of the normal developmental process. Anxiety is the original spur in personality growth, but when this normal process is disturbed by the experience of excessive anxiety, then persecutory anxiety becomes a permanent feature of an individual and creates the most severe kinds of emotional and psychical difficulties.[16]

(2) Depressive Anxiety

Under the influence of persecutory anxiety the infant's ego is still uncoordinated and its objects are partial objects. For an infant the mother's breast stands for the mother. It is an object, not a person for an infant because in an infant's mind it exists totally for the infant's own need. The infant does not yet see it as an object existing in its own right. The infant's ego is still feeble and not yet a whole, so it is easily knocked over by its anxiety. When the ego splits its object into good and bad, it also splits itself into good and bad parts.[17]

As the child's ego becomes more fully organized, the internalized imagos will approximate more closely to reality and the ego will internalize the objects more fully. Its relation to object is being changed from a partial object relation to a whole object relation. The ego also comes to be felt as more whole. Now the child begins to perceive its mother as a whole person. It is during the first three to four months that an infant experiences the persecutory anxiety and its ensuing process. Then with the development of the infant's ego a new kind of anxiety comes into being. Klein called this a depressive anxiety.[18]

Persecutory anxiety persists and plays its part, but it lessens in quantity and gives new way to depressive anxiety in the course of a normal development. Depressive anxiety is the fear about the loss of the loved object whereas the persecutory anxiety is the fear of annihilation. Depressive anxiety is predominantly concerned about the harm done to internal and external loved object by the subject's destructive impulses. During the phase of persecutory anxiety the object, the breast, is split into the good and bad breast. Then the split between the good and bad breast begins to integrate to become a whole object. The ego also comes to be felt as more whole. This integration takes place at the same time with the onset of depressive anxiety. The basis of depressive anxiety is the synthesis between destructive impulses and constructive impulses expressed in the feelings of love toward the object. Under the depressive anxiety the child suffers depressive feelings because its loved person (internal and external) is felt to be injured. Depressive anxiety has manifold contents, such as; "the good object is injured, it is suffering, it is in a state of deterioration; it changes into a bad object; it is annihilated, lost and will never be there any more."[19]

The depressive feeling becomes the source for the guilt and later for the wish for reparation. The ego begins to feel the responsibility for the preservation of the good object or for the restoration of it. It feels sadness for the injured object or for the impending loss of it.[20]

Guilt in its earlier form, however, under the influence of persecutory anxiety and sadism, reproaches the child's ego. The child feels persecuted by its own guilt. The impulse to hate is stronger than the impulse to love in that kind of guilt. Here, hate and sadism turn against the child's ego than outward in projections onto others. This is the phenomenon that takes place in the early phase of the transition from the persecutory state to depressive state. Along with the process of ego development, with the integration of the object as a whole object securely introjected, the stage of guilt proper arrives in the course of personality development.

Guilt spurs a wish that becomes the source for creative activity and restoration of the inner objects.[21] The tendency to make reparation plays an important role in our sublimation and object relations because that is the agent of process of transformation of destructive impulses. Around the time of weaning it can be observed that at times, without any particular external cause, children appear depressed. These are visible signs of reparative impulses operating in children. Klein observes this phenomenon as followings;

> At this stage they try to please the people around them in every way available to them--smiles, playful gestures, even attempts to feed the mother by putting a spoon with food into her mouth . . . With older children, the need to deal with guilt feelings expresses itself more clearly; various constructive activities are used for this purpose and in the relation to parents or siblings there is an excessive need to please and to

be helpful, all of which expresses not only love but also the need to make reparation.[22]

The reparative wish begins in the depressive position with the recognition of attacks made on its primitive form of internal object. In its early phase the reproaches of that object are felt as guilt. In its mature form it develops into a concern for the object that is an ability to carry out the reparative wish. The concern for the object contributes not only to build up the inner objects but also to relate to the external objects more realistically based on reality testing. The concern for the object also plays a role in symbol formation because it helps the child to renounce the omnipotent possession of the object. Instead a symbol is created to replace and to represent the object without being fully identified with it.[23]

Like persecutory anxiety, depressive anxiety is a part of the process of normal development of personality that every child undergoes. Persecutory anxiety develops into genuine guilt and a wish for restoration of inner objects that are the basis for the morality. When the process of transformation of persecutory anxiety is disturbed, however, an extra ordinary amount of persecutory or depressive anxiety, which is responsible for a whole group of emotional difficulties, is unavoidable.[24]

3. Anxiety and *Han*

(1) Persecutory Anxiety and "Wonhan"

As is shown in previous chapter, the concept of *han* has been developed in Korea in two streams of "wonhan" and "jeong-han" conflicting with each other or coexisting One criterion for the distinction between them is the quality of anxiety. If the anxiety involved is persecutory kind, it is "wonhan," whereas if it is a depressive kind, it is "jeong-han." The contents of "wonhan" include grudge, hate, and vengefulness, whereas the "jeong-han" contains sorrow, longing, resignation, and emptiness. Underneath the destructive impulses of "wonhan" exists a belief, in phantasy or in reality, the subject is threatened to be annihilated and victimized by bad figures. Thus "wonhan" calls for a revenge. The bad figures should be annihilated for revenge. These bad figures intensify the persecutory anxiety that is already operative in the person of "wonhan."

In Korean culture, the death instinct has been discussed in relation to the concept of *han*. According to the Korean folk beliefs, death is the ultimate origin of "wonhan." From death "wonhan" is born. The aim of "wonhan" is to bring death to the enemies who brought death in the past in fantasy of in reality.[25] The fear of the "wonhan" is the fear of death. Yul-kyu Kim concludes in his study of *han* that "wonhan" is born from death, grows from death, and yields death. According to him, the "mool-guishin," (water-ghost) is a symbolic figure of "wonhan." "Mool-guishin," a ghost of a drowned person, tries to make others drown by haunting them exactly where it drowned, as revenge for its own death. Then the new victim becomes the new "mool-guishin" and tries to make another drown. In this way the drama of "mool-guishin" continues along with the drama of continuing death. This figure can be understood as a symbolic image of the death instinct and persecutory anxiety.[26]

Bou-yong Rhie finds in Korean fairy tales the evil that is impossible to modify or overcome. The result is always the death of the hero in the story. Here evil is a personification of the death instinct. The understanding of the darkest aspect of "wonhan," which is similar to the concept of death instinct, does not, however, signify the conscious recognition of the existence of death instinct. It only refers to the existence of destructive impulse operating in "wonhan." Klein, too, believes that we experience the destructive impulse unconsciously. It operates in us and influences our phantasies and behavior, but we do not know about it. It can be observed that the anxiety of "wonhan" is persecutory anxiety and its primary fear is the fear of annihilation, whose original source is equivalent to death instinct that is symbolized as "mool-guishin" or other evils in Korean folk stories.

(2) Depressive Anxiety and "Jeong-han"
"Jeong-han" contains the feelings of sorrow, love, self-reproachment, resignation, and emptiness. The Korean word "jeong" means affection.

Compared to the word "ae" that is a more general word for love, "jeong" has more of a connotation of libidinal love. The word "won" means resentment or hate. Thus the confrontation between "wonhan" and "jeong-han" is in essence the confrontation between love and hate, or life and death instincts. *Han* is the mixture of love and hate. When hate gets stronger it becomes "wonhan," when love gets stronger it becomes "jeong-han." But the fluctuation between love and hate, between "jeong-han" and "wonhan," does not occur arbitrarily. In *han* there is an innate tendency to stick to one type of *han*: "wonhan" or "jeong-han" character formation. The transition from "wonhan" to "jeong-han" is a very slow and painful process, during which regression to "wonhan" takes place repeatedly. When the depressive pain of "jeong-han" is felt as too painful, "wonhan" is used as a defensive measure against feeling "jeong-han." Yet, in spite of the tendency to move, there is an opposite tendency to remain in the same circle of "wonhan" or "jeong-han."

"Jeong-han" is a painful emotion, for it laments the injury or death of the loved object. The feeling of "jeong-han" is predominantly a depressive feeling. As depressive anxiety is the fear about the well-being of the loved object, "jeong-han" worries about the well-being of the loved object. In "jeong-han" the basic impulse of hate expresses itself in self-reproach. Instead of being projected onto others, the hate is turned inside. In this way the sadism of "wonhan" is turned into the masochism of "jeong-han."[27]

The feature of the self-reproach is the expression of the immature form of guilt that appears in the stage of transition from persecutory anxiety to depressive anxiety. The harshness of the self-reproach in "jeong-han" becomes reduced along the course of its maturation into the guilt proper, which is capable of taking responsibility based on a more realistic assessment of reality.

The element of the sense of resignation in "jeong-han" feeling is another sign of an immature "jeong-han," in which the acceptance of reality as well as hope cannot be maintained. By accepting reality, one ends his or her clinging wish, regret, or self-reproach, and assumes responsibility. But in resignation hope is given up. There is a qualitative difference between resignation and accepting reality. Immature "jeong-han" contributes to the "status quo" by giving up all hopes and the desire to create a new reality, whereas mature "jeong-han" contributes to the creation of a new reality by realizing its hope based on reality. Mature "jeong-han" is able to accept fate courageously as the will of God, and by doing so it transforms fate into an *amor fati*.

Klein's theory of two anxieties sheds some light on the nature of original *han*: "wonhan" and "jeong-han." Yet, since *han* is a larger concept than anxiety, a concept larger than anxiety is needed to address the nature of *han* more comprehensively. This larger concept can be found in Klein's "position theory." In her thought the anxiety is part and parcel of a psychic reality, which she called "position."

4. Two Position Theory

According to Klein, there are two positions in personality development and therefore two ways to conceive of psychological disturbances. These are the paranoid-schizoid position and the depressive position. These are originally the two basic phases in the process of personality development that every child goes through, but when fixated they become positions, the bases of the personality disturbances. The position theory is a complex one in which many aspects of psychic activities interact together dynamically. It includes the aspect of anxiety, the ego's relation to objects, and the ego's defense mechanisms.[28]

(1) The Paranoid-Schizoid Position

Based on the clinical evidence emerging from her work with disturbed children, Klein assumes the existence of an innate sadistic impulse, which is the reaction to the persecutory anxiety arising from the death instinct. The child's ego, which exists from birth, experiences anxiety and uses defense mechanisms against it to protect itself from the threats. The primitive ego is also capable of primitive phantasy that forms the contents of the child's inner world. Phantasy is the mental corollary, the psychic representative of the instincts that operate from birth.

When the child first relates to its mother it relates not to the whole person of the mother but to the mother's breast. Its object is a part object instead of a whole object. For the infant, the mother's breast stands for the mother. Later, when the child becomes four or five months old, a change takes place, the infant changes from relating only to the part object to the recognition of the whole object, from the prototype of the breast to the mother as a person. Klein sees the child's relation to the breast as of fundamental importance. It is the first step in building the infant's inner world.[29]

The anxiety at this first stage is felt as persecutory anxiety. Since the primitive ego is very weak and still unintegrated, under the impact of primitive anxiety it tends to fragment and to disintegrate. It fears the total disintegration and annihilation of itself. This fear, which is the primitive ego's reaction to the death instinct, is projected onto the object (the breast) and makes it a persecutory object, which in turn substantiates the primitive anxiety into persecutory anxiety.

The ego, feeling threat from the presence of the death instinct, splits off and projects the death instinct outward as a defense measure to protect itself. With this projection the life instinct that operates in the child from birth is also partly projected. As a result, the first object, the mother's breast that receives projections of both the death and life instincts, is split in two: the persecutory part and ideal part.[30]

The persecutory part is perceived as plural because it is fragmented into many pieces by the death instinct when it is projected, while the ideal part is felt to be whole and intact. The ego tries to protect itself by identifying itself with the ideal object while keeping a distance from the persecutory objects.[31] In this process not only the object is split but also the ego itself. Schizoid mechanisms are used by the ego to defend itself from the threat of the persecutory parts. Splitting keeps distance between good parts and bad parts. Thus the first object becomes a split object. The good object is idealized as a defense measure against the danger of persecutory objects. The mechanism of introjection is used to introject the good part and to build the good inner object inside the ego. When these defense mechanisms cannot defend the ego sufficiently, the defense mechanism of omnipotent denial is used against the fear of persecution. With this defense mechanism the child, in phantasy, totally denies the psychic reality of its fears, and, in phantasy, annihilates its persecutors.[32]

Besides these primitive defense mechanisms--projection, introjection, splitting, idealization, and omnipotent denial--Klein formulates the concept of a new defense mechanism: projective identification. Projective identification is a primitive form of projection where the child projects not only impulses to objects but also parts of the self and bodily products of the child, and identifies these impulses and parts as belonging to the object. The child, in phantasy, believes its projections are part of the object's identity. But then, parts of the child's self are lodged in the object and, if extreme, the child feels it must control the object and that the object can control the child.[33]

In her paper "The Importance of Symbol-Formation in the Development of the Ego" Klein shows how Dick, a four year old boy, equates his sadism with his bad feces or penis. This phenomenon is the evidence for the projective identification through which the child identifies itself with what it projected and also what is projected with the object. Projective identification operates also in its relation to the life instinct in the formation of a good object. When the child's inside is felt to be full of badness the good parts of the self may be projected into an ideal breast, given to the object for safe-keeping.[34] With projective identification not only parts, but the whole self, may in phantasy be projected into an object. This leads to a taking over of the other's personality. This projective identification underlies the psychotic delusions of being another person.

Klein also explains in another paper, "On Identification," that projective identification is the basis of narcissistic object relationships. When good parts are projected in projective identification, there is a strong need to depend on the object because the child's ego is dependent on the good parts. The object has to be controlled, because the loss of the object would mean the loss of a part of oneself. Where there is a need to control the object, there is also a fear of being completely controlled by the object. Here is the root of the schizoid fear of loving.[35]

Under the influence of projective identification, loving means projecting good parts of the self into the object, and depleting oneself and feeling controlled. This is the inner state of the schizoid person who avoids any loving relationships with others. The child flees to an excessively idealized internalized object from the external real object. Then his ego is so depleted by projections that it may become a mere shell for such internal objects.[36] When anxiety is paramount, the child even denies the fact that he loves the object at all. The result may be a stifling of love and turning away from the primary objects, and an increase in persecutory anxiety, i.e., regression to the paranoid state.[37]

Klein does not treat the schizoid position as an independent psychic position but as part and parcel of paranoid-schizoid position. This does not mean that she views the schizoid position as identical with the paranoid position. She seems to consider the schizoid position as a regressed state from depressive or persecutory anxiety, which takes place in the transitional phase from persecutory position to depressive position.

In her paper "Notes on Some Schizoid Mechanisms" Klein describes the psychological dynamics of the schizoid position, which is similar and related to paranoid position. The violent splitting of the self and the excessive projection are the two main defense mechanisms in the formation of schizoid position. Since the destructive and hated part of the self is violently split off and projected outward, introjection of that part into the self becomes extremely difficult. At the same time, because the good parts of the personality are also split off and projected, the good parts of the personality are felt to be lost, which results in weakening and impoverishing the ego. Without having enough goodness in the self to rely on, the ego feels a need for an over-strong dependence on the external representatives of one's own good parts. Then introjection may be felt as a forceful entry from the outside into the inside in retribution for violent projection. In this way the process of introjection, which is of vital importance for the internalization of good inner objects, may be severely disturbed. In the earliest relation to the good object, the ego tends to idealize it. In anxiety situation the child is driven to take flight to his internal idealized object as a means of escaping from the dangers. As a result the ego may be felt to be completely an empty shell for it.[38]

Schizoid people shrink from people to prevent both a destructive intrusion into others and the danger of retaliation by them. They hide from people and avoid relationship with them. They lack interest in people and things. They are marked with artificiality and lack of spontaneity.[39] Most of all they lack the ability to feel genuine feelings.

The real experiences of the baby with its mother greatly influence the early ego's relationship with its internal and external objects. When the baby is hungry, it experiences the fear of persecution as if it was invaded by persecutors and threatened by annihilation. In this state the lack of the good object is felt as an attack by bad objects, because there is no difference between frustration and persecution. With the good experiences of the mother in reality, the child's ego becomes stronger to integrate the split objects, and begins to perceive the object as a whole good object. This whole object is internalized and forms the basis for a healthy personality development.[40]

The features of the paranoid-schizoid position are normal and necessary procedures that every child has to go through during the personality development. The original splitting is a necessary step for developing the capacity to differentiate between good and bad. Projective identification is the basic capacity for symbol-formation and for empathy with others. Only when the normal developmental process is disturbed and the features of the paranoid-schizoid position become fixated,[41] does this position, with its features, become the root for serious psychological disturbances.[42]

(2) Depressive Position

One of Klein's important discoveries in child psychology is that at four or five months a significant developmental change occurs in the infant's life, a change from relating to a part-object to the recognition of a whole object, from the breast to the mother as a person.[43] At the beginning of this stage the whole object, the mother as a whole person, is felt to be the same source both of the child's gratification and of its frustration. The child's love for the mother is therefore very ambivalent and easily turns to hatred. As the child's love gets stronger, it begins to worry about the mother, for it feels she is in danger of being destroyed by its own sadism. This feeling gradually grows into the feeling of guilt.[44]

With the onset of the depressive position, the quality of anxiety changes from the persecutory to the depressive kind. In early stages of the depressive position there is a constant fluctuation between persecutory anxiety and depressive anxiety. It depends on the proportion of hate or love, when hatred is stronger, persecutory anxiety, when love is stronger, depressive anxiety.[45]

Melancholia has its fixation point in the early stage of depressive position, where a child finds himself constantly fluctuating between the two positions, unable to establish securely a good internal object. His suffering is doubled when he suffers self-reproach for the dying or dead good internal object, in addition to the persecutory fears he experiences from the internal and external objects.[46]

The major task for personality development in this phase is to establish in the core of the child's ego a sufficiently good, secure, and whole internal object. When this task fails and fixation occurs, it becomes the basis for mental illness of the paranoid or manic depressive kind. When adults experience the breakdown of their mental health on excessive suffering during their life, they experience regression to the state of their original fixation point. People suffering from depression regress to the early depressive position, in that they have unconscious fear of containing the dying and dead object in themselves. The loss of a loved one in adult life reawakens in the mourner the psychological state of the depressive position. The loved object at a deeper level represents the parental figure, the primary object, which is the basis of his personality structure. With the loss of a good external object, the mourner feels not only the pain of having lost the real external object but also, like the infant in the depressive position, the threat of losing the internal good objects.[47]

Manic defenses are mobilized during mourning. As a defense against the pain of loss, unconscious contempt toward the object and triumphant feeling over it are used, which in turn increases guilt, making the working through process of mourning difficult. The working through process of mourning involves not just the rediscovery of the absence of the object in the external world, as in Freud's concept of reality testing, but also the restoring of the original internal objects with which the lost loved one was identified.[48]

In its early phase of the depressive position the manic nature of omnipotent denial becomes the prominent defense mechanism of ego. With it the psychic reality of depressive pain is denied. Both the dependence on the object and the ambivalent feeling toward the object are denied. Instead, the object is omnipotently controlled and treated with triumph and contempt in an attempt to negate the painful depressive feeling.[49] Suicide is a reaction of manic defenses. While in committing suicide the ego intends to murder its bad objects, it also always aims at saving its loved objects.[50]

The depressive conflict is a constant struggle between the infant's aggression and his love and reparative impulses. The reparative impulse is a wish to repair, make amends, make restitution to make the object feel better, be whole again. In the working through process, destructive impulses give way to reparative impulses. Reality testing is increased when reparative impulses are stronger than destructive ones. The ego learns to give up omnipotent control of its object. External and internal reality become differentiated as the result of the withdrawal of the projective identification that was responsible for the confusion between external and internal reality. Realistic discrimination replaces the split between persecution and idealization.[51]

At the height of the depressive position love becomes stronger and becomes the capacity to recreate the good internal state. Guilt becomes the wish to make reparation to the damaged loved objects. The reparative wish plays an important role for the working through of the depressive position. With the rise of the reparative wish the object, that was previously considered as persecutory, becomes a good object that, in turn, can be used for restoration of the damaged object. In the analysis of a ten year old boy, Richard, for instance, his father's penis in his phantasy, which was a source for his paranoid fear, becomes a tool of reparation. It is now unconsciously identified with his trust in his own constructive and reparative tendencies and is felt to be the most important means of combating the fear of death by being able to create good babies.[52] Along with the overcoming of the early phase of the depressive position, the ego becomes enriched with its internal objects.[53] Klein emphasizes that the ego, with its enriched internal objects, becomes the basis for the formation of a healthy personality.

> A securely established good object gives the ego a feeling of riches and abundance that allows for an outpouring of libido and projection of good parts of the self into the external world without a sense of depletion. The ego can then also feel that it is able to reintroject the love it has given out, as well as take in goodness from other sources, and thus be enriched by the whole process.[54]

The development of the depressive position is the basis for the mental function of symbol formation and sublimation. The ability to form and to use symbol is part of the evolution from the paranoid-schizoid position to the depressive position. For those who are fixated in the paranoid-schizoid position, symbols are completely identified with objects in a concretistic way. Symbolic meaning is beyond their capacity to understand. Only those whose ego maturity reached to the depressive position can appreciate symbols that represent objects without being completely identified with them.[55] The good objects internalized in the self are the imagos of the objects, which are created through the process of symbol formation, than objects in a concretistic way. This becomes the basis for people's capacity of symbolic equation without being fixated to certain symbols.

The depressive position is a phase of personality development during which the core part of personality structure is established. A successful work through of this position is the precondition for the healthy, creative living for a person. If the person has not been able to work through the depressive position during his personality development, he may be exposed to mental illness of the depressive type.

5. Three Position Theory and *Han*

Klein's theory of positions provides a dynamic understanding of the complexities of *han*. The paranoid position and depressive position can be compared to "wonhan" and "jeong-han" respectively. An independent treatment of the schizoid position will add further clarity to the understanding of *han*.

(1) The Paranoid Position and "Wonhan"

Among the common features of the paranoid position and "wonhan," the aspect of paranoid anxiety has already been discussed, and showed that persecutory anxiety was part and parcel of the paranoid position and "wonhan." Along with persecutory anxiety, the ego's relation to the object, and the ego's defense mechanisms involved in the paranoid position, exist and operate in "wonhan." In an explanation of the feeling of "wonhan," Jung-rip Lee, who explicates the philosophy of "Jeung-san" religion, provides insights on the inner dynamics of "wonhan" that can be compared with the inner nature of the paranoid position.[56]

> When one fails to achieve his desired goals after a great effort and struggle, due to an unexpected mistake or any external persecution or intervention, he experiences frustration and disillusionment. Then takes place a split of the consciousness into two parts: positive and negative. The positive part, which carries the thought "it could have succeeded," remains in the self, while the negative part, which carries the thought "it failed because of this and that," brings about despair and regret. Then the feelings of despair and regret are channeled into the stream of regression, which flows backward and fixates at a certain point of regressed state. This is the place of "won" from which, through the vehicle of projection, arises "wonhan," the hate and vengeance toward others.[57]

Jung-rip Lee explains "wonhan" in terms of thought process, whereas Klein pays attention to the phantasy process. Phantasy process is an earlier form of thought process which remains and operates underneath the logic of thinking. Two ego mechanisms are prominent in

Lee's description of "wonhan": splitting and projection. The consciousness is split into good and bad parts, and the bad parts are projected onto others. These two mechanisms belong to the ego mechanisms of the paranoid position in Klein's thought. External persecution is pointed out as the immediate cause of "wonhan." Without mentioning them explicitly, Lee implies that persecutory object relation and persecutory anxiety are the cause of "wonhan." Regression is another important factor in reactivating the archaic ego mechanism. In "wonhan," one regresses to infantile psychology, which exists in the deeper layer of adults' psyche. He is aware of the fixation point in the regressed state of the mind as the location of "wonhan." In fact, his concept of the fixation point is not different from the fixation of the position in Klein's term.

Hate and vengeance are the prominent qualities of the "wonhan" feeling. The hate and vengeance of "wonhan" accompany the phantasy of manic nature; the persecutory objects are ruthlessly annihilated. Ruthlessness is a characteristic of "wonhan," for it lacks concern for the objects. "Wonhan" does not know about guilt. As Yul-kyu Kim points out, there is no place for a super-ego in "wonhan."[58]

Projective identification operates in the phenomena of "wonhan," especially in the symptoms of "sinbyung," in which one identifies with the one who he or she loves or hates, and identifies those parts of self projected into the other, with the other. The four cases of "sinbyung" illustrated by Kwang-il Kim in chapter II show that those who suffer "sinbyung" often identify themselves with shaman or gods of Shamanism.[59] Those who suffer "sinbyung" experience this identification as invasion or possession by the spirit of a dead person or god. When they are healed from it they become shamans who are expert in identifying themselves with those who are already dead, and talk and behave as if they were the dead people. In the rituals of Shamanism, projective identification becomes a useful and creative medium for communicating with an other person's unconscious. This is one evidence of that in the cultural system of Shamanism, the *han* of the shaman is sublimated for the constructive purpose of regulating or resolving other people's *han*.[60]

(2) Depressive Position and "Jeong-han"

The inner dynamics of "jeong-han" are equivalent to that of Klein's depressive position. The most prominent feature in "jeong-han" and the depressive position is that they have love as well as aggression. The main theme of "jeong-han," as it is proved in the long tradition of Korean culture, is love, entangled with hate. This love is not a sweet love, but a painful love. In "jeong-han" the focus is not on the survival of self under the threat of annihilation, but on the well being of the object that the ego relates to. The object is a whole object, and the mother is a whole person. One feels guilt because he feels as if he were responsible for the damage done to the mother. Masochistic self-reproach comes to the fore. There is a feeling of ambivalence toward the object that causes conflict in the self. Struggles between forces of love and hate are acutely felt by the ego. With growing concern for the object, love goes to the object, while hate turns toward the self to preserve the object intact.

"Jeong-han" has two phases in it. In its early phase the tendency of masochism and melancholy is strong. There is an overdose of sorrow and self-reproach. When the pain of "jeong-han" becomes too much, a regression back to "wonhan" easily occurs as a defense measure against the pain. If one is fixated in this early phase of "jeong-han," one will constantly suffer pain and sorrow for an unknown reason.

In its later phase along with the consolidation of ego and its internal objects, the element of self-affliction gradually transforms into a reparative wish. Melancholy is replaced by sympathy for others based on a realistic assessment of them, and it becomes the basis for having a social concern beyond the individual's interest. The sorrow and longing for the loss of the loved object turn into the source for the energy for creating arts. The love in a more mature form of "jeong-han" is better integrated with the aggressive impulse. The love overcomes hate, not by splitting it off and projecting it outward or turning it inward, but by mingle with it and becoming transformed into a new quality of love that can contain hate in it.

This love is distinguished from sentimental love that lacks sufficient realism. Sentimental or melancholic love is a weak love unable to tolerate the aggressive element in it. Thus it splits off the aggressive element and turns it inward. This is the very aspect of "jeong-han" that has been criticized by those who advocates "wonhan." For them, "jeong-han," because of its sentimental and melancholic emotions, is a corrupted form of *han*, so far as it lacks the aggressive energy to struggle against injustice in society and to bring about a social change. The masochistic melancholy of "jeong-han" may deserve criticism, but this criticism does not justify the regressive movement toward "wonhan," which is a more primitive form of *han*. A further development of "jeong-han" into its mature form, and its resolution in its final stage, is a better solution than replacing "jeong-han" with "wonhan."

In its mature phase, "jeong-han" becomes the basis for the concern for others and society. It has not only enough love but also enough aggression to fight against the injustice in society. The quality of aggression that stems from mature "jeong-han" is different from the aggression that stems from "wonhan." The aggression of "wonhan" easily becomes destructive force and destroy objects indiscriminately and ruthlessly. It carries a phantasy of annihilation of the persecutors as the revenge against them. It calls for violence, which in turn calls for more violence, thus forming a vicious circle of "wonhan." A true form of energy for social change or revolution cannot be expected from "wonhan." Only the aggression based on love can be used for the creation of a more humane community. "Wonhan" destroys the individual and society, and calls for more "wonhan"; but "jeong-han" in its mature form heals the wounds of individual and society, and builds a community. When "jeong-han" becomes fully mature it is no longer *han*, but love, which is the genuine power of healing.

(3) The Schizoid Position and "Huhan"

Klein considers the schizoid position a part of the paranoid-schizoid position, where as in the Korean tradition it has been treated as partial attribute of "jeong-han." Yet, a closer examination of Klein's view of the schizoid problem, reveals that she views the schizoid problem as the ego's defensive reaction to depressive feelings, and it takes place in the stage of transition from the paranoid position to the depressive position.[61]

Harry Guntrip examines Klein's works on the paranoid-schizoid position and argues that the paranoid and schizoid problems are different in their characteristics. The paranoid position is fear ridden, but the schizoid position is withdrawing from the burden of dealing with external reality. He asserts that they should be dealt with as two different type of personality constellation no matter how closely related they are. Both persecutory anxiety and depressive anxiety are object relation experiences. While the schizoid position cancels object relations in an attempt to escape from both persecutory and depressive anxiety. Whereas the depressed person turns his anger and aggression against himself and feels guilty, the schizoid person seeks to withdraw from the intolerable situation and to feel nothing.[62]

Guntrip's emphasis on the schizoid feelings of emptiness provides further clarity to our understanding of the feelings of emptiness in "jeong-han." In Korean cultural understanding feelings of emptiness are considered as part of "jeong-han" than "wonhan." "Wonhan" is not compatible with feelings of emptiness, whereas the feelings of sorrow, longing, self-reproach, and loneliness that are the components of "jeong-han," can easily be changed into feelings of emptiness. Seen from the perspective of Korean cultural understanding, Klein is right in that schizoid features are a part of child's experiences during the transition from the persecutory position to the depressive position. It seems however, as Guntrip suggests, that an independent treatment of the schizoid features can bring about further illuminations for the understanding of *han*, especially the *han* of empty feelings.

The emphasis of the aspects of *han* has changed throughout Korean history, along with the change of the reality of life of the people. The main characteristic of *han* during the Yi dynasty was "wonhan," and its fear was the persecutory fear of death. The fall of Yi dynasty and the loss of national independence brought forth "jeong-han," with its depressive feelings and sentimentalism, as the most visible type of *han* among Korean people. In the 1970's, when the problem of *han* began to receive massive social attention among Korean intellectuals, the *han* experience evolved to a new stage, with its emphasis on emptiness. This type is vividly illustrated in Eun Ko's experience of *han*.

> *Han* is the world of emptiness existing in those minds who gave up the operation of their lives of positive will, courage, and adventurous spirit. . .. *Han* is not the emotion of possibility, but the emotion of impossibility. It is not the emotion of hope or dreaming, but that of "I-absence," which can be obtained by the resignation of hope. *Han* is where the beauty of art and the emotion of "jeong" vanish and become nothing, a phase needed to reach the highest state of nothingness.[63]

The world of *han* of emptiness can be named "huhan." The Korean word "hu" means emptiness. Schizoid feelings such as emptiness, despair, hopelessness, resignation, and boredom are the main characteristics of "huhan." Seen in terms of object relations, "huhan" is essentially an escape from both external and internal realities, and flight into the deepest hiding place in the self. People of "huhan" can withdraw so completely into themselves that they may lose touch altogether with their external object world. They may face the danger of depersonalization of their ego along with the derealization of their environment, a psychological catastrophe that may lead to suicide. The "huhan" suicide may primarily be a longing for the union with the idealized inner love object. Although their world of inner objects is impoverished and has become an empty shell, "huhan" people still keep their primitive, extremely idealized inner object imago that they are longing for. For them this inner object imago is a place for a rebirth or an actual death. It is a solemn question whether the withdrawal of "huhan" results in rebirth or actual death.

According to Klein's understanding, the schizoid position, which may be considered as identical with "huhan," is the consequence of the disturbed introjection process due to excessive splitting off and violent projection. What most needed for the schizoid position is the internalization of the good object through the work of introjection. The operation of the reparative impulse in the schizoid position can be most effective in the ego's work of internalization of the objects, if it does not project too much of its own phantasy. With the lessening of persecutory anxiety and repeated good experience of the real objects, the withdrawn ego can be freed from its frozen shell and restart its growing process in the world of object relations.

6. Envy and *Han*

Klein states that, among the factors that interfere with the smooth development of personality from the persecutory position to the depressive position, thus making the working through process of the depressive position difficult, two are significant, one internal and the other external. The internal factor is the instinctual problem inherent in human nature. The external factor is any environmental problems the child experiences during the critical period of early development. The real experience of hunger or separation from the mother causes excessive persecutory anxiety traumatic to the child. The mother plays the most important role in the child's experience of external factors. An excessively narcissistic mother, unable to cope with the infant's projections and keeping herself as an idealized object, puts the infant in a constantly devalued position in relation to herself. In reality those two factors are intricately related and interact dynamically.[64]

Klein's primary attention is paid to the interaction between instinctual factor and the environmental one. Through her work delving into the child's relationship with its first object, mother's breast, she arrived at the conclusion that the most potent factor in undermining the building up of a good object in an infant is envy.

She claims that envy arises in earliest infancy as an expression of the death instinct. In its fundamental primitive form envy is directed at the feeding breast. The milk that embodies mother's love and care, stirs in the infant two opposite reactions: one of gratification (a primitive form of gratitude); the other of hostility and envy. This is done based on the ego's realization that the source of food and love lies outside one's self. Envy can be aroused by frustration and deprivation also. When deprived, the infant may assume that the goodness of the breast is monopolized by the breast itself. In its mind, the breast becomes bad because it keeps the goodness only for itself. This experience of deprivation increases greed, persecutory anxiety, and envy.[65] The infant in phantasy tries to scoop the goodness out of the breast or spoil it out of envy. Klein distinguishes envy from the related concepts of jealousy and greed.

> Envy is more primitive than jealousy; it arises in a part-object relation and is not related to a triangular situation. It is purely destructive and aimed at the object of love and admiration. Jealousy is a more sophisticated feeling belonging to the Oedipal triangle. It is based on love, and the hatred of the rival is a function of the love for the object of desire . . . Jealousy can be noble or ignoble, but envy is always ignoble. Greed also has to be differentiated from envy. Greed aims at possession of all the richness of the object, beyond the need of the self or the capacities or willingness of the object. The damage done in greed is incidental. In envy the direct aim is to spoil the attributes of the object. These are goodness, beauty, and values that are enviable. This spoiling also has a defensive aspect, since, if the enviable characteristics are destroyed, one no longer has the painful experience of the feeling of envy. Thus, spoiling is both an expression of and a defense against envy. Greed operates mainly by introjection; envy by destructive projective identification.[66]

Envy, if excessive, becomes a fundamental factor in the pathology of the positions, paranoid, schizoid, and depressive. In both the paranoid and schizoid positions envy increases and maintains the persecutory anxieties because it destroys the good internal figures that are the resources for overcoming the anxieties. In the depressive position, envy maintains the persecutory aspect of guilt, and adds hopelessness to it. An envious attack on a loved object stirs an intense guilt and feelings of hopelessness. It spoils the reparation. Any restoration of the object to its original state of goodness arouses more envy and becomes a target for an envious attack. Envy mobilizes powerful defenses that interfere with the gradual development from both the paranoid and the schizoid positions to the mature depressive position. An excessive envy makes the split between good and bad so deep and wide that later integration process becomes impossible. When the object is split into an idealized part and an extremely bad part, idealization may serve mainly as a defense against the emotion of envy. Then, with this strong idealization, the capacity to differentiate between good and bad is impaired, becoming responsible for wrong judgement based on phantasy instead of reality. Excessive idealization increases envy, and the idealized object easily turns into an object of hatred and persecution. With excessive envy the mother's breast cannot be appreciated. It becomes a devalued object. Thus the child prematurely looks for another source of gratification. Without having adequate oral satisfaction the child moves prematurely toward genital gratification, resulting in a premature genitality colored by oral sadism. Genitality based on a flight from orality is often the cause of obsessional masturbation and of promiscuity. The lack of primary enjoyment introduces compulsive elements into the genital desires.[67]

Envy has been recognized as a seedbed of *han* in Korean cultural tradition. Yul-kyu Kim includes the envious relationship between mother-in-law and daughter-in-law when he points out the four major factors that contributed to the formation of *han* in Korean people; foreign invasions, political oppression and exploitation, poverty, and the conflict between mother-in-law and daughter-in-law.[68] The core of the conflict between mother-in-law and daughter-in-law is, of course, envy. Envy is also the main theme of the relationship between stepmother and daughter, which is a major theme in Korean fairy tales. "Kongjui-Patjui," a Korean tale parallel to the western Cinderella story, shows that envy is a major cause of *han*.[69]

In the story of "Kongjui-Patjui," the heroine Kongjui was hated by her stepmother and her stepsister Patjui. They envied her beauty and goodness. One day the stepmother gave weeding hoes to her daughters and made them weed the field. To Kongjui she gave a wooden hoe for a stony field, but she gave to Patjui an iron hoe for a sand field. While Kongjui was working hard, her wooden hoe was broken, and she cried, not knowing what to do. Then a black ox descended from the heaven and plowed the field for her. On another day, there was a big party in the town and all were invited. The stepmother and Patjui left for the party after assigning Kongjui a huge amount of work. She had to draw water to fill all the jars, chafe and cook the rice, and weave fabric on a loom. This time her animal friends, sparrows, toad, and ox appeared and helped her to finish the work. Then, a "seonyu" (an oriental angel) appeared and gave her pretty clothes and shoes. Wearing these, she left for the party. On the way home, she lost one of her shoes. It was found by a noble man who began to search for the owner of it. Patjui tried the shoe, but her foot didn't fit it. When Kongjui tried it, she fit perfectly. The noble man, pleased with Kongjui, proposed marriage, and the proposal was accepted. A wedding ceremony was arranged. Out of envy Patjui and her mother poisoned Kongjui and killed her. Patjui, disguised as Kongjui, was sent for the wedding. The dead Kongjui, yet, was resurrected as a lotus flower, then transformed into human again, and told everything to the noble man. Patjui and her mother were punished by death. Kongjui married the noble man and lived happily ever after.[70]

In this story envy is depicted as the wish to kill the source of beauty and goodness. It is a poison to spoil. It causes innocent suffering, and contains the wish for revenge. As the story shows, the *han* of Kongjui takes revenge against Patjui and the stepmother with death. In Korean folktales the element of envy is considered as a major cause of *han*.

CHAPTER IV

THE *HAN* OF THREE INDIVIDUALS

1. King Yonsan and "Wonhan"

(1) Historical Records of King Yonsan's *Han*

In Korean history the *han* of King Yonsan is a well-known case of individual *han*, with its catastrophic consequences to the people and to the history of the nation.[1] The following descriptions of King Yonsan's *han* are based on historical data recorded at the time by court scribes and others. Some original records are written in Chinese characters, which were used in official writings in those days. These have been translated into modern Korean by historians.

Yonsan was born the first son to King Sungjong and Queen Yoon, and had right of succession to the king. Around the time of Yonsan's birth a conflict arose between the king and her wife, because she was jealous of two women--Soyong Jung and Sookeu Uhm--who Sungjong favored as his concubines. One day when Sungjong visited the Queen's room to see and hold the newborn baby he was rejected by the Queen. Using the baby as a weapon, she tried to force her husband to give up his relationships with the two women. After this incident the king ordered the baby to be sent to Lady Ahn to be cared for. Lady Ahn was

57

Using the baby as a weapon, she tried to force her husband to give up his relationships with the two women. After this incident the king ordered the baby to be sent to Lady Ahn to be cared for. Lady Ahn was known among high society then for her virtue and noble character. This took place when the baby was three or four months old. The queen was devastated by the forced separation from the baby, and she became extremely aggressive toward her husband.

Then the second incident took place. It was found that the queen was hiding poison in her room, and she was placed on house arrest. The baby was still being nursed on the queen's milk that had to be delivered to Lady Ahn several times a day.

Finally, the third incident occurred when the milk for the baby was found to be tainted. It was revealed that the mother herself did it with the intention of taking back the baby, thinking that if the baby became sick due to the sour milk it would be returned to its real mother.[2]

After this series of incidents, the queen was deposed and sent into exile. This happened when the baby was about a year old. From exile she waited three years to be called back by her husband. Instead she received what she never had imagined,--an order to drink poison. So she died with *han*. This was when the baby was four years old.[3]

Yonsan grew up under the care of Lady Ahn without knowing his real mother. It was forbidden to let him know anything about her. He liked his godmother, Lady Ahn, who took good care of him. Two scholars were chosen to be his teachers, Ji-suh Jo and Chim Huh. Their teaching styles and personalities were very different. Jo was strict and admonished the prince with strong words; Huh was lenient and let Yonsan follow his pace in his studies. Yonsan liked Huh and hated Jo.[4]

During his adolescence, knowledge of the violent aspect of Yonsan's personality began to spread throughout the royal court. One episode that revealed his violent feature occurred when he was visiting his father's court and was welcomed by the deer, which was the king's favorite pet. When it approached him to express its affection, he kicked the deer sharply in the belly. Sungjong caught his son in the act and reprimanded him harshly. Yonsan was silent, but he didn't forget this incident.[5] When he became the tenth king of the Yi dynasty at the age of nineteen, he shot the deer with an arrow and killed it.[6]

One day King Yonsan came upon a record, in the royal history, of his mother. It revealed that the deposed Queen Yoon had been put to death. Yonsan called in his three highest ranking ministers one by one to find out what it meant. No one dared to reveal the secret about the late queen, fearing its tragic consequences. All three resigned from office, and they were followed by the resignations of dozens of other officers. With the help of Sa-hong Im, a notorious opportunist, Yonsan eventually discovered the truth about his mother's death in the records of "Wangjo-silrok" (The history of the dynasty). He also found out that his maternal grandmother was still alive in the countryside, and he sent people to fetch her. His grandmother confided to him the details of his mother's dying moments, and she gave him a piece of cloth stained with his mother's blood. His mother's final wish was that her death be avenged against those who were responsible.[7]

All this happened during the first year of his reign, but he refrained from taking any action regarding his mother's death. After a while, he began to be haunted by the *han* of his mother, and the seed of her vengeful wish started to germinate quietly deep in his mind.

The Yi dynasty was founded on Confucianism, an elaborate system of political, ethical, and moral principles. Confucian scholars held the main positions in the king's cabinet, giving advice to the king regarding the proper ways of ruling the nation. Yonsan disliked these scholars because of their constant criticism, and he felt his freedom being threatened. There were others, as well, who hated the scholarly group, for their political ambition. Ja-kwang Yu and Geug-don Yi took advantage of Yonsan's dislike of the scholars, and accused them of injecting an unorthodox view into the royal history. They insisted that the writings of Jong-jik Kim, who had been the leader of the cabinet until his death, contained criticisms of king Sejo[8] for stealing the throne from his young nephew, Danjong. The innocent scholars were arrested, imprisoned, tortured, and killed. About thirty well-known scholars were killed solely because they had been disciples of Jong-jik Kim. Yonsan ordered "Bukwanchamsi" (dismemberment of the body) for Jong-jik Kim who had already died. This was the "Muo Scholars Massacre" (1498 A.D.), one of two massacres during the reign of Yonsan.⁹

The second massacre was the "Kapja Scholars Massacre" six years after the "Muo Scholars Massacre." The second massacre was the direct consequence of Yonsan's avenging his mother's death. Ten years after discovering the secrets of her death, his vengeance was abruptly ignited, when his maternal grandmother urged him to punish the two women who had once been rivals of the late Queen Yoon. With renewed rage, he ordered them brought to him and he beat them to death. Their two sons, who were Yonsan's half brothers, were flagellated and sent into exile. Then later killed. In an attempt to stop the murder of the former king's women his paternal grandmother was violently pushed by Yonsan and died of shock soon after. Twenty six scholars and their family members were killed or, if already dead, disinterred and dismembered. Among twenty six, eight were received "Bukwanchamsi." Several thousands lost their lives during this massacre.¹⁰

Apart from the two massacres, many other instances betrayed the pathology of Yonsan's personality. Remembering his hated childhood teacher, Ji-suh Jo, Yonsan tortured and killed him by grinding his body with a grind stone. At the time Jo had been living quietly in his hometown in the countryside. He had given up all of his high positions, and knew that Yonsan's destructive personality would stain the whole country with innocent blood. Meanwhile, Chim Huh, a figure reminiscent of Yonsan's benign mother, was idealized and after a series of promotions became a high minister.¹¹

Yonsan's extreme suspiciousness was revealed in several instances. Once he ordered "Sungkyunkwan," the center of education and a mecca for confucian scholars, closed out of fears that he was being spied upon by the students from over the wall. No one dared to oppose this idea because Yonsan had become an absolutely terrifying figure then.¹²

His paranoid fear caused him to demand an evacuation of the citizens around his hunting grounds, thousands of people lost their homes in a single day without getting any compensation. Ironically, the most feared despot was trembling with fear of his people. One of them wrote a letter of protest in "hangul," the Korean script. In those days it was considered to be the script of uneducated people and women, while Chinese characters were highly esteemed as the script for educated people. Thousands of people were tortured in an attempt to find the complainant to no avail. The angry Yonsan proceeded to ban the use of "hangul" and to collect and burn all the books written in "hangul."[13]

Yonsan's promiscuous sexual life added even further tragedy to the lives of many of his people. He indiscriminately raped the wives of his subjects no matter how high their rank. Many of them committed suicide out of shame. He raped female monks in the temple during the day, and he even raped one of his aunts, who later committed suicide. His greed for women knew no limits. Several thousand pretty women, married or unmarried, were conscripted from all over the country to be his concubines.[14]

During the Yi dynasty, Confucianism was the national religion and the others, such as Buddhism and Shamanism, were repressed. Shamanism especially was looked down upon as an irrational, superstitious religion good only for women, who were treated inferior to men. It was considered a disgrace for a king to have any relationship with a shaman or shaman-related affairs, but Yonsan liked Shamanism and frequently brought shamans into the court to do rituals. The closed "Sungkyunkwan" was used for this purpose. During the rituals, Yonsan would be possessed by spirits and danced with the shamans, behaving as if he were a shaman himself. He even suffered a mental illness similar to "sinbyung," an illness of shamans-to-be. Dong-shik Ryu, a pioneer in the study of Korean Shamanism, finds in the story of Yonsan the oldest remaining record of "sinbyung." He believes that Yonsan was on the verge of becoming a shaman, if not already one. He reports as follows;

> King Yonsan suffered a madness for several years. Waking from sleep with shrieks, he ran into the back yard until he became exhausted. He enjoyed "kut," a shaman ritual, and became a shaman himself with singing and dancing. In rituals he was possessed by the spirit of his dead mother, the deposed Queen Yoon.[15]

Yonsan's *han* is typical of "wonhan," with its main elements of aggression and vengeance, and the consequences were tragic. The whole nation was devastated morally and economically. With the corruption of the central government, the abuse of power by local authorities was even greater. Finally a few courageous people, led by Won-jong Park and Heu-an Sung, stood up against Yonsan. The rebellion was successful on account of the full support from the people. Yonsan was dethroned and sent into exile until his death.[16]

(2) The Inner Dynamics of King Yonsan's "Wonhan"
Despite that the two tragic massacres were related to the power struggles among political groups, historians agree that Yonsan's personality was more responsible for the massacres than the power struggle.[17] Yonsan's personality was manipulated by one political faction to destroy the major political power group, resulting in the Muo Massacre. The Kapja Massacre was the direct product of Yonsan's "wonhan."[18] It was his revenge for his mother's "wonhan." The first massacre was not so different from the second in its psychological dynamics, for both massacres could be understood to be the result of the "acting out" of Yonsan's unconscious phantasy. Yonsan's *han* contributed to the social and political disaster of his reign, which in turn burdened the people with *han*. In the Muo Massacre, Yonsan's interest was to get rid of those who, both in his phantasy and in reality, were constantly critical figures, what Klein would call persecutory figures. In the Kapja Massacre, he identified with his mother's "wonhan," but it was his own "wonhan" that he had projected onto his mother.[19]

A prevalent belief among people regarding Yonsan's *han* is that "wonhan" was begotten in his mind after his discovery of the death of his mother and her "wonhan." This discovery must have disturbed his psyche, deeply arousing its archaic contents. His mother's "wonhan" reawakened his own "wonhan," which was in the deeper layer of the psyche. Yet, his "wonhan" existed long before the discovery of his mother's "wonhan."[20]

A. Oedipus Complex

An intense Oedipal feeling was clearly exposed when Yonsan kicked belly of the deer, his father's favorite pet. In such a scenario Yonsan's feelings of rivalry with his father were transferred to the deer. Because he knew his father's power, he could not express these feelings directly and instead had to suppress them until his power increased. On the very day he became king, he shot and killed the animal with his hands. Seen in light of the Oedipal theory Yonsan was killing not just an animal, but his father. Yet, his feelings were far from those of the Oedipus complex proper, as he felt no regret about it. Historical records show that he felt pure hatred, with no trace of love, toward his father.[21] The Oedipal conflict is primarily a triangular relationship between the parents and the child; in Yonsan's case his mother-figure was absent, and his relationship with his father was not one of rivalry, but of persecuting father and persecuted son. The death of his father didn't arouse feelings of mourning or guilt, but a feeling of triumph. The Oedipus complex, therefore, is a concept inadequate for a complete explanation of Yonsan's *han*. It shows much more primitive features than that of the Oedipus complex.

B. Persecutory Fear

Yonsan seems to have been driven by his paranoid fear. It compelled him to annihilate those who were faithful to him. He feared them, and to him they were persecutory figures. He perceived their professional advice as a threat to him. In the Kapja Massacre, his persecutory fear got form as he projectively identified himself with his dead, persecuted mother. In reality, it was probably his persecutory fear that he attributed to his mother. Out of his paranoid fear he closed down "Sungkyunkwan" and evicted the people from their homes. His fear extended even to the written language itself, when he banned the use of "hangul" and also burned all the books written in "hangul."

C. Fragmented Ego-Objects

Yonsan's way of fighting his enemies was to tear them limb from limb, literally to make them into parts. In Klein's theory his object relations never reached the level of becoming of whole object relations. It seems that in his unconscious phantasy, his objects were fragmented into many pieces. Thus, in making his phantasy a reality, many people had to be killed. "Bukwanchamsi" was his favored punishment for the dead. While for the living his favorite means of execution was "Neunjichucham," a dismemberment of the living. For him, not only bad objects were fragmented, but so were good objects. While he desired pretty girls, they were not different from dispensable things. He was driven to collect several thousand girls, so that the good objects in his life might outnumber the bad.

D. Splitting

A major element in the inner dynamics of Yonsan's *han* was splitting between the good and bad. This splitting was always so deep and wide that an integration of both aspects into a whole was impossible. For him, the good seemed extremely good and idealized, while the bad was extremely bad and persecutory. To him, anyone who contradicted his wishes, was extremely bad. This split was evident most dramatically in his relationship with his two childhood teachers, in that he projected a good part of himself onto Chim Huh, and bad part onto Ji-suh Jo. Chim Huh was an idealized mother figure to him, while Ji-suh Jo was a bad persecutory mother (or father) figure. This psychological mechanism of excessive splitting is responsible for his inability to distinguish between right or wrong, true or false, which in turn caused so many innocent casualties.

E. Projective Identification

Projective identification, which is Klein's concept referring to one aspect of the psychological dynamics of the paranoid-schizoid position, is evident in the *han* of Yonsan when he identified his "wonhan" with his mother's "wonhan." During the shaman rituals, his total being became identified with that of the shaman and, at other times with that of his dead mother.[22] These instances of total identification with other personalities show that Yonsan's basic way of relating to an object was through projective identification and the most primitive form of object relation. The features of Yonsan's *han* correspond to the inner dynamics of the paranoid-schizoid position.

(3) The Aetiology of King Yonsan's "Wonhan"

Yonsan suffered few traumatic experiences of deprivation, or physical or emotional abuse, as a child, while he was under the care of Lady Ahn. Historical sources suggest she reared the future King with the best of care. Actually, King Sungjong would sometimes express his thanks for her excellent care of the prince with generous gifts and valuables. Yonsan was gentle in Lady Ahn's care, further proof of her estimable reputation. She was the only person to whom Yonsan paid respect during his lifetime, and despite that he hated one of his two teachers, he seemed to have enjoyed his childhood and adolescence. The only thing he lacked during this period was knowledge about his mother, which was the national secret.[23]

The wounds in Yonsan's personality, therefore, must have taken place during his infancy, when he was separated from his mother at the age of four or five months. The crucial period during which the transition from the paranoid-schizoid position to the depressive position supposedly takes place. This abrupt separation from his mother, with its ensuing anxiety must have been a traumatic experience for the baby. With the separation he lost his mother's breast, his first object, while he was still nursing. He lost his mother's face that he could recognize and appreciate. Thus, no matter how good his foster mother was, the anxiety he suffered must have been enormous. If he experienced excessive anxiety at this stage, the fixation point in his personality could be in the paranoid-schizoid position, because his continuity of being was disrupted even before he could reach the depressive position in the process of personality development.

The origin of Yonsan's *han*, yet, may go even further back to the period of the first few months after birth when he was in the care of his mother. Maternal care in this period is crucial for the child's healthy development of personality. The mother's physical and emotional health are indispensable for a sound start in the maturation process of the child. As Klein discovers, the infant in this phase has to go through all the features of paranoid-schizoid position; fear of annihilation, persecutory anxiety, sadistic impulse, fragmentation of the ego object, and envy. The transition from the paranoid-schizoid position to the depressive position can be successfully completed through the infant's repeated experiences of goodness and gratification in relation to its mother. The historical records show a strong possibility that the baby Yonsan had an extremely difficult infancy in relation to his mother even before the separation.

The behavior of Yonsan's mother during the period of her early motherhood suggests that she was in an emotionally disturbed state because of her intense jealousy of her husband's concubines. Her reaction that when her husband tried to hold the baby she snatched it away from him, may be understood as the expression of her envy. When the King arranged a foster mother for the baby, his supposed rationale was to protect the baby from potential damage by its mother. Further research is needed to figure out whether he took the baby away from its mother because he sensed a destructive impulse in her, or as punishment for his wife's defiant behavior. At any rate, the separation from the baby exacerbated the mother's emotional condition to such a degree that her jealousy degenerated into primitive envy, which essentially is a wish to kill. She obtained poison as her weapon to kill but it was discovered by the King upon the house search. She explained that it was to kill herself. Her explanation aroused more fear and suspicion about her sanity among the people around the King. When she attempted to regain her baby by making it sick with tainted milk, she must have been so blinded by the intensity of her rage that she could not see she risked taking the baby's life. The poison and sour milk can be considered as two concrete examples of Queen Yoon's envy.[24]

Klein views envy as the most potent force that can cause the fixation in the early developmental position of paranoid-schizoid. Although the envy Klein cites is the envy in the infant and not that in the mother, her insights about the role envy plays while creating fixation of the position are illuminating to the understanding the origin of Yonsan's *han*. According to her, the envy of the infant is a normal and natural element in its instinctual energies, and unless it is excessively strong, it is gradually overcome by the repeated experiences of satisfaction and love in the infant's relationship with the mother. Only when the infant is genetically endowed with excessively strong envy does the process of overcoming the envy become extremely difficult.[25] Compared to the envy of the infant, however, envy in the mother is much more detrimental in its consequences. The infant's envy can be contained by the mother's indestructible goodness and love, and can thus be modified and overcome. But the mother's envy cannot be sustained by the infant. If any strong envy in the mother operates in her relationship with her infant, the infant has to defend itself from this envious attack. The only defense in this stage is identification with the envying mother. The infant, in an unconscious phantasy, has to destroy or spoil the mother's breast by scooping it out or inserting something poisonous. The envy of the infant can be seen as its defense against the envy of the mother, making the infant's envy excessively strong. Then, the process of child development (from the paranoid-schizoid position to the depressive position, through the establishment of good internal objects in the child's ego), cannot proceed smoothly, and it becomes fixate in a primitive stage of personality development. Klein believes that envy is the ultimate source of disturbance in the development of sexuality and causes compulsive masturbation or promiscuity. In this regard, Yonsan's promiscuity and compulsion to rape in his adult life may be seen as the result of the excessive envy he experienced during the symbiotic period between mother and baby. Since there is no evidence of genetically endowed excessive envy in the baby Yonsan, his mother's envy, spurred by the injustice done by her husband, and the male-dominant political and social system, can be considered as the decisive element in the aetiology of Yonsan's *han*.

2. Sowol and "Jeong-han"

Sowol is a national figure of "jeong-han" in Korea, who is loved and remembered for his poems of "jeong-han."[26] For Koreans, Sowol is symbolic name that represents the poems of "jeong-han," not just a pen name for Chung-sik Kim, the poet. Sowol's *han* is different from Yonsan's in many ways. Sowol's *han* belongs to the category of "jeong-han" in which love is stronger than hate, while Yonsan's *han* belongs to "wonhan," in which hate is stronger t*han* love. The medium for Sowol's expression of *han* was poetry, through which he expressed his subjective experiences of *han*, whereas Yonsan's *han* was expressed through the political actions by "acting out" unconscious phantasies in real life.

(1) Sowol's Poetic Images of *Han*

> "*Han*"
> *Han* is loneliness
> sorrow
> empty feeling of hunger
> anguish or sadness.
> *Han* is at once lyric,
> at another tragic longing
> even excruciating pain
> entangled with regret
> or self-reproach.[27]

In this poem the whole picture of "jeong-han" experiences is depicted as a chunk of feelings, containing many different kinds of feelings such as loneliness, sorrow, emptiness, anguish, longing, pain, regret, and self-reproach.

> "In the night"
> It is really lonely to sleep alone.
> In the night I am sorely longing for my sweetheart
> exceedingly like this.
> I'm afraid lest I forget even her face.[28]

Sowol's *han* in this poem is the feelings of loneliness and longing for his loved one. Sowol's sweetheart in reality is unknown. She might be someone existing only in his inner reality. He still loves her and longs

for her even after he loses her. He worries about his fading memory of
her and does not want to let her image disappear, as he invested so
much of himself in it.

> "The word of *nim* (Thou)"
> For three years time was running like a stream
> and the water in the pot is decaying,
> but your voice is still whispering;
> "Shall we walk together?"
> Your voice is like an arrow piercing my living heart.[29]

In this poem the poetic image of *han* for Sowol is an arrow piercing
his heart. Three years have passed since he lost his loved one, and his
heart is like water decaying in the pot because of sorrow. Yet his
memory of her words continually renews the pain of losing her. For
him, *han* is a wound caused by the loss of the love object, and it is a
painful wound that cannot be relieved by the passing of time.

> "The word of *nim*"--(continued)
> Spring grasses are returning to life in its season,
> but like a tree cut down from the bottom,
> like a bird with both wings broken,
> my body will never bloom again.[30]

In this verse Sowol's *han* is felt as hopelessness. He likens himself
to a cut down tree or a bird with broken wings. The self is not totally
dead yet, but it is gravely wounded or even dying. Apparently, unlike
other poems of Sowol in which he is concerned about his loved one, in
this poem he is concerned about himself. In a deeper level, however, he
is still concerned about the loved inner-object. His self is identified with
its endearing object that is seriously injured and dying. Sowol is
depressed and feels deep in his heart the injured or dying object.
His inner object is not totally dead yet, but it is gravely injured that
there is no hope for restoration.

"A lump of sorrow"
Like burning incense in the jar,
kneeling down in prayer,
I see a small lump of sorrow in my heart.
Like weeping rain drops in the shade of early moon,
a small lump of sorrow in my heart.[31]

In this poem *han* is a small lump of sorrow that is symbolized by the image of burning incense. Unlike images of the felled tree or the bird with broken wings, the image of burning incense does not invoke a mood of hopelessness but a solemn religious mood. From the incense burner scent is being emitted, transforming sorrow into solemnity. *Han* is not like the rain drops of a shower, but like those in the shade of the early moon. It weeps not as an open cry, but as silent tears. It is sorrow deeply suppressed in one's heart. If it can be exploded in a blazing fire or in a rainy storm, it is not the *han* of Sowol. It is deeply suppressed sorrow, which becomes also the source of his religious yearning for his eternal "nim" (Thou).

"A song of sad love"
You are a willow tree whirling,
reflected on the surface of the water in the river,
whirling and whirling in the wind
endlessly.
I am the leaves of the tree
suffering endlessly because the tree is whirling,
withered and withered till the leaves are falling.
The falling of leaves in the season is
because of the frost and the west wind,
but I am falling alone
still green because of you.[32]

In this poem, Sowol depicts the relationship between the loved one and his poetic self. His loved one is like a whirling willow tree reflected on the surface of the water, a beautiful expression of his inner image of his beloved. Like an image reflected on the surface of the flowing water, his inner object is so fragile that it easily breaks into pieces. He equates himself with the leaves of the tree that suffer and fall because the tree is whirling. A modicum of aggression can be detected when he blames the frost and the west wind for his untimely death. He feels himself dying while still green, unable to live his life fully. This image of the falling green leaves can be seen as a poetic image for Bou-yong Rhie's idea of *han* as "unlived life."[33]

> "Evocation"
> A name shattered to pieces!
> A name scattered in the void!
> A name that never replies!
> A name that I'll die calling!
> . . .
> Turn me into stone,
> I'll call your name till I die.
> My beloved!
> My beloved![34]

The cultural context of this poem is a funeral ceremony, in the early part of which the spirit of the dead is called to be present in the ritual. Then the *han* of the spirit of the dead is reactivated to be pacified and resolved. The mood in this poem is much different from that of the other poems in that it is not suppressive but explosive. The loved object is fragmenting into pieces and is scattering in the void. Traces of the fear of fragmentation of the object can be seen in this poem. The poet's inner object is shattered and vanished, but still he cannot stop loving it. Thus his pain of love continues without knowing its end.

> "Judpong bird"[35]
> Judpong
> Judpong
> awrabi judpong[36]
> My sister, who used to live by the Jindoo River

is now crying in the village
by the Jindoo River.
In the old days, my country
in the far-away vales,
My sister who was living by the Jindoo river
was killed by her stepmother's envy.

Shall I cry out for my sister?
Oh! the burning sorrow
My sister who was killed by the envy
became a Jupdong bird.
Her nine brothers
she could never forget, never forget.
In the dead of night
when the world is asleep,
she cries mournfully, flying
from mountain to mountain.[37]

In this poem the poet's *han* is depicted as the *han* of the sister who died because of the envy of the stepmother and became a jupdong bird. Although it shares the common root with the envy contained in the "Kongjui-Patjui" fairy tale,[38] the nature of *han* in this poem is different from that of "Kongjui" in the fairy tale. Unlike the *han* of "Kongjui," the *han* of the sister in this poem does not seek revenge against the persecutor. The only concern of the jupdong bird is about the young brothers she loves. She cries mournfully, unable to do anything for them.

"Azalea Flowers"
When you hate to see me
and decide to leave,
I'll quietly let you go.
I'll pluck an armful of azaleas
in the Yaksan hills at Yungbyun
to strew over your path.

Tread softly on the flowers,
each step soft and silent.
When you hate to see me
and decide to leave,
I'll never, never shed tears.[39]

In this poem, the azalea becomes the image of *han*. The pain of separation from the loved one is symbolized by the image of the azalea being crushed by the step of the leaving lover. Separation from the loved one is always painful, but in this poem an extra amount of pain is involved because of the aggression turned inside. A masochistic tendency is contained in Sowol's *han*. He cannot let his lover go without scattering azaleas, the poetic image of his heart, on the road. "Jeong-han" always contains a certain amount of aggression in it. In a healthy "jeong-han," aggression is better integrated into love. Thus aggression can be expressed toward the object in a healthy way. In a less healthy "jeong-han" it is suppressed by the love for the object and turned toward the self. An example of the healthy "jeong-han" can be found in the most famous of the Korean folk songs, "arirang," in which a modicum of aggression is freely expressed toward the lover who is leaving.

"Arirang"
Arirang arirang arariyo
climbing up the hill of arirang
My "*nim*" who is going away leaving me behind
will get a foot ailment before going "simri"[40]

(2) The Inner Dynamics of Sowol's "Jeong-han"
The feelings of Sowol's "jeong-han" encompass a variety of feelings of loneliness, longing, remorse, emptiness, sorrow, and helplessness. These interact dynamically to create an emotion that can be considered the uniquely Korean emotion of *han*. Thus when *han* is considered as a feeling of complexity, it specifically refers to "jeong-han" than "wonhan," which has somewhat simple emotions of revengeful

aggression and fear. Despite all the diversities and complexities of the feelings and images involved in "jeong-han," it does have a basic structure around which a myriad of combinations may be clustered. At the core of the basic structure of "jeong-han" lies the endless pining for the lost love object. The poet is lonely, sad, helpless, remorseful, and empty because of the "*nim*," his loved one, who is absent, weeping, separating, dying, or dead. In its basic structure Sowol's "jeong-han" can be understood as equivalent to Klein's idea of the depressive position.

Both in "jeong-han" and depressive position, the anxiety involved is depressive anxiety, which is distinguishable from persecutory anxiety. In depressive anxiety the main concern is about the fate of the love object, whereas in persecutory anxiety the concern is about the fate of the self. Klein describes this with clarity as follows;

> I came to the conclusion that persecutory anxiety relates predominantly to the annihilation of the ego; depressive anxiety is predominantly related to the harm done to internal and external love objects by the subject's destructive impulses. Depressive anxiety has manifold contents, such as; the good object is injured, it is suffering, it is in a state of deterioration; it changes into a bad object, it is annihilated, lost and will never be there any more.[41]

An early form of guilt is an element involved in the process of identification with the injured inner object. Sowol seems to feel he is responsible for the injury of the object, and that he should be punished and made to suffer on behalf of the love object. Thus his suffering has an element of masochism. His sorrow is mixed with remorse and self-reproach. As is shown in the poem "Azalea," the poet wishes to be crushed by the steps of "nim." This masochistic tendency makes his poems melancholic or sentimental. This early form of guilt is apparently not yet clearly recognized as the tendency to make reparation. However the tendency to make reparation to the lost object already operates beneath the more predominant features of melancholy. His poems can be understood as the result of the tendency to make reparation, through which he is constantly trying to create the image of the loved one. This feature of Sowol's poems shows that the fixation point of Sowol's personality is in the throes of the depressive position, as he is unable to work through it completely.

The synthesis of the two opposite impulses of love and hate is the basis of depressive anxiety. In Sowol's "jeong-han," as in his poem "Azalea Flowers," both elements of love and hate are contained; but the hate is turned toward himself and forms the basis of masochism while maintaining the innocence of the object. The verse "When you hate to see me and decide to leave" conceals and also reveals the poet's own aggression toward himself. The synthesis of love and hate is achieved to some degree in his "jeong-han," but it is still in a premature stage in which the tendency to split the love and hate still operates preventing a better integration.

Both in the depressive position and in "jeong-han" the object involved is a "whole object" instead of "part objects." In Sowol's poems, his "nim" represents a whole object, a loving person. The Korean word "nim," a heavily culturally loaded word, always means a whole object than a part object. Seen from Klein's theoretical framework of personality development, this feature implies that during the process of personality development in early childhood, Sowol's ego was able to integrate the "part objects" into one "whole object" to some degree. Somehow though, before the process of establishing the inner object was completed, a psychological injury might have occurred so that the inner object remained as an insecure, injured object. As Klein finds, even during the depressive position in which the more integrated ego introjects and increasingly establishes the whole person, persecutory anxiety persists. During this period, the infant experiences not only grief, depression, and guilt, but also persecutory anxiety relating to the masochistic tendency; defenses against persecutory anxiety exist side by side with defenses against depressive anxiety.[42]

The main defense mechanisms operating in Sowol's "jeong-han" seem projection and introjection. He uses them in the formation of poetic images. Repression is used to hold the sorrow deep in his heart, to form "a small lump of sorrow." The differentiation between good and bad, object and self, is made, and there is no trace of confusion caused by the operation of projective identification, which is, according to Klein, the most prominent mechanism of the paranoid-schizoid position. The split serves to keep the ideal object separated from the aggression rooted in the self, as illustrated in the poem "Azalea Flowers" in which the aggression is turned toward the poet himself. It is in Sowol's poem "Evocation" that a trace of paranoid fear can be found through the poetic images of fragmented object in the void. When the pain of the loss of the object becomes unbearable, a temporary regression from the depressive position to the paranoid-schizoid position takes place, and paranoid-schizoid mechanisms are used to deflect the pain from depressive position. The best defenses against the pain of the loss of the whole object are to fragment the object, the cause of pain and sorrow, or to deny the psychic reality of the pain. Thus, the subject feels as if he were merely an empty shell. This feeling of emptiness is the end result of the series of the depressive position. This is the psychological situation in which one easily succumbs to the temptation of suicide, as Sowol did and died when he was 32 years old.[43]

(3) The Aetiology of Sowol's "Jeong-han"

There is no detailed description of Sowol's early childhood except a few important clues to the aetiology of his *han*. He was born as the first child to a wealthy family in 1902, and he must have had a smooth and happy life during his first year. For unknown reasons, his father became mentally disturbed by psychotic symptoms when Sowol was one year old. His mother, who had been very devoted to her child, had to leave the baby in the care of his grandfather because she had to take care of her husband. As Mog-wol Park, a well-known Korean poet, finds the origin of the *han* of Sowol in this tragic family environment of his early life,[44] it can be said that the baby Sowol must have been traumatized by the sudden loss of his love object, his mother when he was one year old. In Klein's scheme, this trauma took place in the developmental stage of the depressive position and became a permanent fixation in Sowol's personality. Sowol's grandfather seemed to enjoy taking care of the baby, and Uhk Kim, in his writings about the life of

Sowol, describes an aspect of Sowol's grandfather's caring of the baby. "His laughter of joy used to resounding throughout the town while he was watching the baby who was looking at the world with its frightened eyes, lying in the swaddling cloth."[45] Sowol's grandfather could be a good substitute mother, but it seems that the baby Sowol could not find his lost mother in the eyes of his grandfather.

3. Eun Ko and "Huhan"

(1) The Fantasy World of Eun Ko's "Huhan"

The exploration of the *han* of Eun Ko is significant in this study, because he not only interprets the *han* of the people but also explores his personal *han* sincerely through his literary activities. He has played a central role in the Minjung movement, a Korean people's movement emerged during the struggle for democracy and human rights against the military dictatorship of the 1970's and 1980's.[46] He provides records of his inner experience of *han* in his essays published in 1971. In that year, he went through a period of introspection during which he experienced in his mind an explosion of thoughts and images that he detailed in one hundred thirty four letters to an imaginary woman. This period can be viewed as one of creative illness during which a reactivation of his unconscious materials took place. He was hiding in a place, a nearly deserted, small temple located on the high mountain near the city of Seoul, when he wrote about his fantasies. These fantasies are the expressions of his inner world of *han*.[47]

In his fantasy, the city from which he escaped is described as a deserted place where no human voice can be heard because there is too much noise. It is a dangerous place, filled with sadism, where no ethics can survive except the ethics of despair.

> Thus you are living in a state of hopelessness. In that city the only ethics is the ethics of despair. It is like a huge psychiatric ward where even the doctors are insane.[48]

Because the city is felt hopeless and insane, he does not want to return to it alive or even in the form of a ghost after death. He not only withdraws from the city but also wants to erase all the trace of himself in the city. In this fantasy he feels the persecutory fear and wishes to withdraw from the reality to a hidden place.

> I will never go back to your city. Please burn every trace of
> me remaining in the city if there is any. Even my ghost will
> not go back to the city . . . I want to get rid of the memory
> of myself. I did not exist from the first.[49]

The defense mechanism of denial is operating in this thought process when he denies his body, memory, and even his existence. Still he has a paranoid fear of the city lest it sends people to his hiding place to arrest him.

> Somebody is after me. In the thick fog I hear the hushed voice
> of the searchers who seemed to find the trace of me . . . I
> believe that you didn't inform against me. But I am being
> searched for. If I were arrested by them I might commit
> suicide before they drag me away.[50]

This hiding game is not a game, for it lacks element of play or joy. Persecutory anxiety spoils the playful elements of the game and make it a matter of life or death.

Though he hates the city, he does not want it to disappear, or to become a better place to live. He wants it to stay the way it is, because he needs something to criticize and negate in order to feel alive himself.

> I do not want your city to become an ideal place. Because I
> can live most of all by criticizing your city. I cannot live
> without negating something. . . . I negate all including
> myself. I am achieving the confusion of negation.[51]

He identifies himself with the temple where he is hiding. The image of deserted temple is a poetic expression of the emptiness of his heart. He feels himself as an empty shell, deserted by the whole world.

> I am becoming the deserted temple . . . It is myself. The
> emptiness of my heart appears as a deserted temple.[52]

This empty place where he is hiding is not a secure place. He feels
insecure in the temple because emptiness fills it. The danger of the
emptiness of the temple is greater than the danger of the city because he
feels the danger of losing the image of his loved one in that emptiness.

> It is dangerous to exist alone in this space. Emptiness is more
> dangerous than my inner and outer world . . . A vast empty
> space is erasing your image in me.[53]

To him the image of the loving one is more precious than anything
else, and it must be defended from the danger of being erased by
emptiness. He identifies with the emptiness because the best defense
against the enemy is to ally with it. Thus he becomes a nihilist who
advocates emptiness and despair.

> The best literature must containnihilism, for it meets with
> despair creatively. Nihilism is the content of despair. you may
> accuse me of being a despair maniac . . . My despair is all
> my health . . . You and I should spread the religion of despair
> in the world. Ah, I am the disciple of despair. I wish you
> would become the Mary Magdalene of despair.[54]

He not only identifies with despair that he fears the most but also
elevates it to the level of religion. The basic motif involved here is to
defend the weak ego from the hopelessness and despair. When he lacks
hope that can be used in defending against the despair, he paradoxically
tries to overcome the despair with despair.

> Despair can be liberated only by a deeperdespair. I tell you
> this repeatedly. It is a must. Only an idiot does not despair .
> . . If there is a boy who is the symbol of hope, you have to
> kill him and go inside him.[55]

In fantasy he kills the boy who represents hope, and goes inside him. The mechanism of projective identification, in Klein's terms, is operating in this fantasy. He not only projects his destructive impulse onto others but also identifies with it. Thus, destruction is not only justified but also idealized in the name of creativity, freedom, history, and even humanity.

> Do not be afraid of destruction. The one who fears no destruction has the will to create. If you fear destruction you cannot create anything. Then you become a slave who obeys the will of political power . . . History proceeds through destructions. Through many destructions humanity should be born again.[56]

The idealization of destruction is followed by feelings of guilt and depression. Here arises a need to idealize the feelings of depression. Idealization is a strong defense against the feelings of depression. When there is no goodness remaining in the self, the final defense against the feelings of depression is the idealization of them.

> Without the depressive feeling you cannot live. It is a life that lives not just one generation but beyond the generations . . . I wish you spread the sickness of depression in your city.[57]

This is a tragic situation that is denied triumphantly. Tragedy is depicted as something desirable and needed, because it can function as defense against the feeling of nothingness. Tragedy always evokes in the minds of people strong feelings of fear, awe, hate, and sadness.

> Tragedy is what we need. I cannot live without it. I am begging for it. Curse, hate, and condemnation are my personal assets. But I cannot stand in front of nothingness which buries all my assets.[58]

A vicious circle is formed in this mental situation. Having escaped from destructive impulses into emptiness, he has to escape again back to those impulses and becomes trapped in a tragic situation, which is also denied triumphantly. In this process his aggression is intensified and becomes explosive, and, in this psychic situation, images of the explosion arise.

> The moment of ecstasy takes place in my mind when something visible transforms into something invisible . . . I see the whole mountain is burning in flame. I feel the feeling of Nero when he set fire to the city of Rome . . . I burned the mountain here and there. In flame the mountain became the most sublime place. Before I knew no solemnness of mountain like this. Yet, the flame was burning inside me . . . I became hateful of the autumn, so I burned it.[59]

His moment of ecstasy is the moment of burning in flame in which something existing vanishes into nothing. The image of destruction that has become the source of his enthusiasm falls under the logic of the revolutionary idea.

> I am gripped by the logic of extremity which becomes the logic of revolution. The logic of revolution is exclusive and destructive and without which a new reality cannot be achieved. I love indescribably words like extreme, utmost, ultimate, etc.. I am aware of their destructive function and of the possible bankruptcy of mental health involved in them. But, I have the most contempt for the words such as moderation, midway, or golden rule.[60]

His fantasy of revolution is a defensive reaction against the threat of emptiness. He chooses to destroy it because the image of his inner object is threatened by emptiness that can erase it or swallow it up. Emptiness is the arch enemy against the image of the inner object, which is the only and most precious asset of himself. This object is under the threat of being erased by emptiness.

> I can relate to you only by hypothesis. If the fake word "dangshin" (you) were not permitted, this writing would be

meaningless . . . I am an absentee from you. The word
"dangshin" signifies emptiness.[61]

Because the inner image of "dangshin" is so precious to him he has
to preserve it. In an attempt to preserve the image of the love object, he
wishes to transform the image of 'dangshin'[62] into ash, because to him
ash is the final thing that is sure to survive the destructive impulses
symbolized as burning.

> "Dangshin!" Ash! Why don't you become ash and fly over to
> me? Ash is pure no matter what its previous form was. You
> will become ash when you die. Take your clothes off and
> touch your body. It is tomorrow's ash. Love is not a pink
> color, but ash.[63]

His mother image is colored with intense hatred and contempt. This
negative mother image can be seen as aspect opposite to that of the
idealized inner object--"dangshin." In his unconscious the mother image
is split into two, ideal and contemptible.

> I have no parents. I have nothing . . . I will eradicate
> emotions such as "Ah mother!" and encourage to have only
> fatherly love. I like Jesus because he called his mother,
> "woman!" . . . I hate the mother's soft voice, saying, "Are
> you coming now? You are late." . . . I scorn the soldier who
> dies calling for his mother.[64]

He does not explain why he hates and has contempt for the mother.
It is something beyond his reason. Moreover, his hate and contempt
toward his image of the mother extend to all women except his
"dangshin." In fantasy he views that women are responsible for all the
evils in the world, which shows the inner world of a misogynist.

> Women are the representative of evil bred by the city. They
> are representative of culture and the evil. It is because of

women that some areas in the world are always under
destruction. I would like to become a man who treats woman
as he treats dogs and kicks them away.[65]

Beneath these negative aspects of his psyche exist the positive
aspects of love and creativity. He feels thrilled and ecstatic not only in
the moment when the object vanishes because of the hateful and
destructive impulse but also in the moment of recreation of the object
out of love. He clearly acknowledges the importance of building inner
objects.

> When one loves an object, he revolutionizes the image of it.
> It appears as a miracle in his inner world. This is the omega
> point of human excitement . . . By loving the object carefully
> as if it is the loving person, and by becoming brother of the
> object, one creates an inner reality that remains in the memory
> for a long time.[66]

In Eun Ko's fantasy there are two ultimate points of alpha and
omega. The alpha point is the moment when the object vanishes into
nothing, whereas the omega point is the moment when an inner object
is created by loving relationship with the external object. He feels
excitement in both moments of destruction and creation. The
consequences of the excitement, however, are much different; one leads
to destruction and death, the other to creation and life. As a person of
"huhan," the *han* of emptiness, Eun Ko needs excitement, an intensified
feeling in order to offset the predominant feeling of "huhan," the feeling
of emptiness and of being unreal. It is plausible that he, in fantasy, has
no choice but to resort to the negative, to feel the sense of real and
excitement, through destruction. At this stage of his personality
development persecutory anxiety seems still to operate strongly, and his
ego is still too weak to sustain the pain of guilt. In his fantasy his love
impulse emerges only after his destructive impulse. For example, he
feels his love toward the beauty of the mountain only after he burned it,
making it ash in his fantasy. A feeling of guilt, an indication of

reparative wish, is not yet seen in this scene of his fantasy. It is important, though, to notice the existence and operation of the reparative wish in its early form in the midst of the expressions of destructive impulses in Eun Ko's fantasy.

But when the struggle to create inner, good objects is repeatedly overridden by the rise of feelings of emptiness, he finally decides to commit suicide in his fantasy. First he transforms himself into an invisible ghost and enters the city to confirm that it is entirely under the blessing of death. Then he goes to the room of his lover to end his life.

> Perhaps I would be dead with a knife stabbed in my chest in your room before you awake. I will enter your room to see your sleeping face and realize that your face answers for everything. Confirming that the word "upanishad" means "the one who is with me," I will stab my chest very quietly. I will keep you in my memory for a long time as my "dangshin."[67]

(2) The Inner Dynamics of Eun Ko's "Huhan"

Eun Ko's experience of *han* exhibits some features of the paranoid position (and of "wonhan"). His attitude toward the city reveals a paranoid type of anxiety because he feels the city is a place filled with sadistic impulses. In Klein's terms, the city represents the mother's belly, filled with bad objects in the phantasy of the infant. Klein finds that at a certain stage of early development the child imagines the mother's belly to be full of sadistic objects such as a penis, mouth, human excrement, etc.. As a defensive measure, the infant splits off the destructive impulses and projects them onto an outward reality.

Projective identification is operating in the phenomenon of Eun Ko identifying with the temple and the temple with parts of himself. He projects his emptiness onto the temple and, at the same time, identifies with the temple. Thus the emptiness of the temple becomes the emptiness of his inner self. This mechanism is also shown in his fantasy of killing the boy who symbolizes hope, and going inside him.

With these ego mechanisms overlaid on the paranoid position, the most prominent feature of his *han* is emptiness. Eun Ko's *han* can best be understood as illustrating "huhan," literally the *han* of emptiness.

The feeling of emptiness is the emotional concomitant of the schizoid mechanisms of the ego. If one cannot bear the bad object relation, let alone the good object relation, he shuts himself off from the object relation itself. In his fantasy after the retreat from the city representing external reality Eun Ko finds his inner world empty because there are no inner objects, good or bad. It is striking feature that the image of his mother is so vague that he feels as if he never had one.[68] He suffers from the vagueness of the image of his loved one. Seen from the perspective of Klein's object relation theory, this loved one represents the ideal part of his mother image. The primary object that becomes the basis of the child's personality structure and remains as a permanent basis for all later object relations in adult life is always the mother or mother figure. For Eun Ko, this image of object is so feeble that it cannot be protected from the fear of emptiness, which is felt to be more dangerous than the sadistic impulses. In the face of the threat of emptiness, he reacts by resorting to the negative object relation. He criticizes the city, destroys it in fantasy, hates mothers, and has violent contempt for women. He prefers feeling bad but strong, than weak and afraid. He does this for two purposes, to defend himself from the danger of being erased.[69] Then a persecutory fear, aroused by sadistic impulses and their accompanied fantasies, becomes so unbearable that he has to try to hide from object relation in a state of emptiness. Thus a vicious circle of the negative object relation and the no-object relation is formed in the schizoid *han*.

The defenses used in this situation are of a manic nature. For Eun Ko, the flight from weakness to manic omnipotent power seems to the fundamental defense than a secondary one. This is shown in his contempt toward women and mothers, which is rooted in his fear of women, especially his mother. His contempt stems from the split part of himself that he projected onto women. It seems that when he criticizes "jeong-han" as a corrupted, womanized emotion, his criticism stems from his fear of women. His contention that the original form of *han* was the wild, male, aggressive emotion of the northern continent of ancient Korea than the tamed, female, passive emotion of the southern peninsula, reveals his contempt of female sexuality.[70] In Eun Ko's "huhan" the manic defenses are potent mechanisms, hampering the transition from the paranoid-schizoid position to the depressive position. His ego is not able to accept its depressive state. It should simply be denied. The depressive mood has to be replaced by the triumphant feeling. Despair is overcome through deeper despair, and aggression by stronger aggression. Finally death is overcome by death. The most dramatic version of manic defense against the depressive state can be found in Eun Ko's fantasy of committing suicide.[71]

In Klein's view, in committing suicide the schizoid ego intends to murder its bad objects, while trying to save its loved objects, internal or external. She states;

> To put it shortly; in some cases the phantasies underlying suicide aim at preserving the internalized good objects and that part of the ego which is identified with good objects, and also at destroying the other part of the ego that is identified with the bad objects and the id. In other cases, suicide seems to be determined by the same type of phantasies, but here they relate to the external world and real objects, partly as substitutes for the internalized ones.[72]

At the heart of Eun Ko's "huhan" lies the mystery of paradox. His death fantasy in the final letter is, of course, the expression of his unconscious wish to return to his mother's womb, which is symbolized as the room of his loving person where he finds the ultimate peace. Therefore, his death could be the sign of ultimate withdrawal from life. Yet, that is not the whole truth. The real meaning of this final action is hidden in the paradox that he obtains, through death, a new life that is real and liberated from the old ties of suffering relationships. His suicide is an action out of despair for his old false life, while also an action of hope for the new, true life. Where there is despair his hope starts. Where only ash is left, he finds love. At the place of his death his new life begins. He titled these letters "Being Transformed, Where Shall We Meet?" It testifies a process of rebirth through death.

When Eun Ko states that "*han* is the world of emptiness that exists in the minds of those who gave up the operation of their lives of positive will, courage, or adventurous spirit," the word "emptiness" does not simply mean a sense of futility. It means love, a pure love. This love, different from sentimental love that should be burned to be transformed into true love, is contained in the *han*, which he calls the highest state of nothingness. But no matter how high the state of nothingness is, and no matter how pure the love of *han* is, there is in reality a great danger of the destruction of the total self, both body and mind. Despite the paradoxical meaning of his words, the contents of Eun Ko's fantasy and his statement of *han* reveal the pathological danger of the schizoid position, and signals a need to be healed.

(3) The Aetiology of Eun Ko's "Huhan"

In his autobiography "The Son of Red Soil," Eun Ko starts his story with his mother's memory of the few days after his birth. He feels this memory very important, because it is about the earliest moment of his infancy.

> According to my mother's recollection, when she came out of the room holding me the day after my birth, the first remark of those women in the town was that I was like a butterfly. I was born as a butterfly. Only two days after giving birth to a white butterfly my mother had to go out to the field to weed, carrying on her head a huge basket of food, which she cooked with barley that she milled herself. Only two days after the delivery . . . Because of that she had to wash five pairs of underwear due to the bleeding after childbirth.[73]

Eun Ko was born fragile as a butterfly and suffered hunger from his earliest infancy. The absolute poverty forced his mother to go out to work, leaving the baby at home. His own memory testifies the similar situation. His earliest recollection of his childhood is about the period when he was still dependent on the mother's breast.

> For a baby, mother and mother's breast are one . . . Mother has not returned home yet, though the barking of the town dogs' was heard. Meanwhile, I was exhausted after a long cry for milk, holding on the skinny back of my aunt, attached to

her like a motionless gadfly. I could cry no more. I could not
sleep either. With an empty stomach you cannot have a real
sleep. It is a sleep of death, which cannot be distinguished
from death or life.[74]

The primary experiences of life for Eun Ko were the absence of his
mother, and hunger. As he clearly recognizes, the absence of mother
and hunger were not two different experiences. Even when his mother
was present her milk was always insufficient. Because of experiences
like this, he had to learn to withdraw from the pain of life to the state
of feeling nothing, which he later called "a sleep of death." After
weaning he spent most of the time alone in the empty house where he
would play alone and fall asleep. When he awoke alone he would cry in
fear of the sky and the earth, which he felt had suddenly enlarged
enormously. The cry for his mother was heard by no one, and stopped
only from exhaustion.[75] His experiences of early childhood objects were
all related to the element of emptiness, absence of the mother, empty
breast, empty stomach, empty house, empty heaven and earth.

Eun Ko finds the aetiology of his *han* in the environmental factor
surrounding his early days of life. He recognizes that the mother and
infant relationship is the matrix of the basic formation of the personality
as well as of personality disturbances. Although he knows that his
mother was the most important factor in the formation of his *han*, he
does not consider his mother as the origin of his *han*. He finds the
decisive factor for the genesis of his *han* in poverty. In the foreword of
his autobiography he writes, "I grew up in the poverty that was larger
than mother or heaven."[76] To him poverty is a bigger problem than the
mother-infant relationship, because he finds that poverty was the reason
he suffered the absence of the mother who was everything for the infant.
He thinks his mother would have been a good mother, if only she had
been released from the spell of poverty. Because of the living conditions
dictated by poverty, she was unable to devote herself to the needs of her
baby.[77]

For Eun Ko, poverty means more than just the lack of material
objects. It was his world and his reality. He suffered from the lack of

an object, the primary object, right after birth so that the process of the internalization of the object could not proceed smoothly. As the result, "the schizoid position" was formed in his personality. When he says, "self is not lost but is hidden deeply in ourselves as an inner being, waiting to be rediscovered by those who are searching for it,"[78] the insight comes from the introspection of his schizoid type of self.

(4) The Transformation of Eun Ko's "Huhan"

Eun Ko left his home at seventeen, right after the Korean war. He had lived the life of a bohemian for years, before he became a Buddhist monk and retreated to the mountain, withdrawn from the secular society for ten years. He could not find inner peace in the temple, even through the practice of stringent self discipline.[79] His diary entries written during twenty one days of fasting shows the sincerity of his self discipline. He returned to society as a poet and writer, and continued his search for his true self in the secular world. He seemed, during this period, more dependent on the aggressive impulse in his critical writings on various subjects, than the creative impulse. Only after the reconciliation with his mother did his creative impulse come to the fore, transforming him and the quality of his writing. For the twenty years since he had left home, he had completely cut himself off from his family. One day not long after his return to secular society, he had a dream of his father's death. Two days later, he received a telegram stating that his father had died. This news shook him hard, and the inner wall he had constructed against the memory of his childhood could no longer hold. He came home to attend the funeral and there found his mother, not the mother he hated and held in contempt in his unconscious, but the mother he could love in reality. Before this, he had negated his mother's love, degrading it as something ugly, contemptible, and childish. In an essay for mother's day he had once written an article for a newspaper, titled "Throw away your mother on mother's day."[80] Seeing his mother again changed his attitude, and he confessed in the later essay, "My mother," how he felt sorry about his previous writings about mothers. His dreams reveal his genuine guilt toward his mother.

> These days, though this is a shameful story, I return in my
> dreams to a childhood in which I defecated in my pants on the
> way home from school . . . and at home I got a spanking by
> my mother. Being awakened in the middle of sleep, after
> drinking a little cool water, I cry helplessly looking at the
> dawning sky through the window.[81]

With this dream he could recall a real memory of his childhood
incident. Out of extreme shame and humiliation he could not cry then.
Only when he could forgive his mother, thirty years later, could he cry
over that incident.[82] In his later essay, "Mother is Boddhi-Sattva,"
published in 1987, his mother image gets the attributes of the Holy
Mother.

> Therefore, though she is the mother of a nameless
> street-person, mother is related to Boddhi-Sattva and is the
> container of love representing the Holy Mother . . . Because
> this world is made by the love of all mothers, in spite of all
> the   suffering   afflicted   by   ugly,   devilish,   desolate,
> dehumanizing reality and poverty, diseases, and oppression,
> the world finally becomes the place for joy, forgiveness, and
> love. Without the love of the mother this world cannot sustain
> itself even for a moment. Thus, mothers are more   than
> mothers. They are the Boddhi-Sattva for the billions of
> people.[83]

His rediscovery of the mother led to the repair of his childhood
memories of his hometown. His autobiography, "*The Son of the Red
Soil*," was the product of his reparative wish to restore the inner objects
of his childhood life. In his book of poems, titled "*The Story of Ten
Thousand People*," he extended his love to the people of his hometown,
and restored the image of each one of them in the poems.[84] His creative
contribution to the Minjung movement in Korea lies in that he rescued
the meaning of the word *minjung* from becoming a faceless,
depersonalized aggregation of people designated by sociological,
economical, and political categorization, by giving each person a unique

name and personality, having their stories. The personalization of *minjung* is the result of his reparation toward those figures of his childhood, whom he held in contempt and treated as worthless. They are not figures any more, but people he loves and are a precious part of his inner world.

His idea of self is community-oriented, *minjung* oriented, in which he finds not an individualistic, closed, isolated system, but a potential space large enough to include people. It is a space open toward the community, and exists in the webs of relationships with other *minjung*. His mother is perceived as a Boddhi-Sattva who is manifested in each person of *minjung*. His primary object, the mother, is transformed into an object spacious enough to contain thousands of objects, *minjung*. This transformation has its prototype in his memory of the first sublimation of his mother in which, as a baby, exhausted from waiting for mother and food, he found the stars shining in the summer night sky and asked for them to eat, as if they were food. He recalls, "To me sky was my mother, the "namunjai" (an edible wild plant) field where my mother worked, and the stars in the sky were my fruit and food. It did not come through my mouth, but through my eyes."[85] The stars in the sky he had seen in his early childhood become the faces of his hometown people in his poems, "*The Story of Ten Thousand People*." According to Klein, the appearance of genuine guilt which accompanies the reparative wish is the crucial sign of working through the depressive position in the process of achieving a healthy personality. This takes place only when the good objects, especially the good mother, are securely internalized in the self. Then, guilt is transformed into the creative urge to heal and recreate the damaged or lost objects. Works of art or literature can be produced during or after this process.

In Eun Ko's case the recovery of his real mother was the momentum for liberation from his schizoid shell in which he had been hiding. What he found back home was his real mother who simply touched his head and said, "This is my child." That night he slept in his mother's bosom, touching her breast as if he had become a baby again. He rediscovered the mother he had lost in his infancy. Since then his healed self, with its creative energy, expressed itself in productive literary and social activities. In 1976 he had a dream that shows the inner world of his self, filled with abundance of good and healthy inner objects.

> Last night I dreamed of a huge open square. It was not the square of yesterday. It was a beach of a river. I was not sure whether it was the Han river, the Dooman river, the Nakdong river, or the Yongsan river.[86] The beach was very spacious and was by the flowing river filled with clean water. Gathered there were all fifty million Korean people, male and female, young and old. There were people selling foods, soup and rice, noodles, cakes and fried fish, etc.. Every one of them was smiling brightly. They were discussing the future of the nation and the people. Among them was Koo Kim who was assassinated. There also were Joong-keun Ahn, Dong-sam Kim, Yong-woon Han.[87] My father was there, too. As someone shouted, "Where is the way that leads us to life?," all the rest of the fifty million people responded in one voice, shaking the foundation of the earth, "It is right here." I also shouted with them.[88]

This dream shows a picture of a mature, healthy, and creative inner world of personality. He is no longer in a closed inner space, but in an open square. The darkness of *han* is replaced by the brightness of the beach and of the smiling faces. The emptiness was filled with people and their voices. Elements of female and male are well integrated. There is enough food, which represents the creative energy for life. The objects of his idealization--the national leaders and his father--are in his inner world. In this dream, he finds a new meaning of his life; his vocation. The new goal for his life is the unification of the nation. His journey to overcome the "huhan" and its empty feeling in the self is over, and a new journey to overcome the nation's *han* has started. This journey is very different from the previous one. Instead of empty feelings he feels joy. Instead of withdrawal, he participates and fights not with hate but with love. In his square, "any person of closed darkness can receive in his mind the shining love of the square."[89] This was the vision that made Eun Ko a *minjung* poet and a leading figure in the Minjung movement in Korea.

(5) Social Implications of "Huhan"

The social implication of "huhan" is grave. People with schizoid problems are most vulnerable to social epidemics. Since "huhan" has emptiness in the personality, it is exposed to collective infections. People with "huhan" tend to become nihilistic, hiding themselves behind the mask of a great cause, ideology, or philosophy. Because the emptiness of "huhan" fills the core part of themselves, they are unable to hold any values. This nihilism is the greatest threat to the effort of building a society based on human values, for by its nature nihilism cancels the very fabric of human society by negating human values. In the fantasy of Eun Ko's "huhan," the tendency toward nihilism can be seen when he hails nihilism as the best part of literature.[90]

The logic of the thought of schizoid people tends to be extreme because they are unable to sustain any kind of ambiguity that may evoke feelings of confusion and helplessness. They have to choose the strongest words and the most extreme lines of activity as a defensive measure against their own fear and contempt for their weak existence. Therefore they are easily "gripped by the logic of extremity," as in the fantasy of Eun Ko.[91]

An effective escape for schizoid people from their feelings of emptiness and boredom is the flight to the negative object relations, because the bad object relations can be a temporary relief for those who suffer the lack of any object relations. They involve themselves in aggressive and destructive behavior because only in that kind of destructive activity can they feel they are really living. David Holbrook, a Cambridge professor emeritus who used Guntrip's and Klein's theories, among others, to examine culture and the arts, expresses this phenomenon succinctly;

> So, he or she either conforms to a "social" identity in a
> nervous, automatic way, or, tries to distract the self from the
> problem of emptiness and compulsive activity, or becomes
> aggressive, as defense measure. Such False Self activity, if
> taken up by a group of people, seduced into assumed strength
> in fear of inner weakness, can become a collective

> infection--especially if a group of schizoid people take the
> ultimate flight-path from the love they fear, and give
> themselves over to the joys of hating and get what pleasure
> they can out of that.[92]

"Huhan" people try to justify destruction and violence in the name of future creation, so they become revolutionaries. Their interest is not in the creation of something valuable, however, but in the destruction itself, for they have no hope for the future. Hopelessness and despair are their plight. The more desperate task for them is to defend themselves from their feelings of emptiness by joining in violent social action.

Extreme idealization, of someone or of a certain cause, is a feature of the "huhan" phenomenon. This is an attempt to vitiate one's feeling of worthlessness by identifying with the idealized object. "Huhan" people feel they have something more valuable than anything else, than even their lives. Any frustration, despair, or disillusionment during their struggle for the great cause may cause an explosion of rage in committing suicide. They tend to idealize and praise suicide in the name of the great cause, and avoid looking at the tragic aspect of the death. For them, the life of an individual is less important than the solution of the social problem. They even sacrifice themselves in suicide. But "huhan" suicide is a false solution for the problems of society, let alone the problem of the individual. It only brings more tragedy, not only to the individual involved, but also to the whole society.

Eun Ko is right in his assertion that, with their *han*, *minjung* cannot remove social contradictions. He believes that only the overcoming of *han*, through the scientific understanding of it, can bring about the beginning of a new history for the society. By the overcoming of *han* he means the overcoming of nihilism, sentimentalism, powerlessness, and submissiveness. He concludes that *han* has to be sublimated into the energy for the world of love.[93]

Only when the *han* is overcome, can it contribute to the society as a true form of creative energy. To become the "world of love" which Eun Ko advocates, both "wonhan" and "huhan," as well as the immature and sentimental "jeong-han," have to be transformed into the true and mature *han*. This transformation process is the process of healing of the original wounds. The original wounds cannot be magically healed. They may remain as a permanent source of pain and suffering for an individual. Yet, through the healing process, a transformation of the quality of their nature takes place. Therefore, the belief that the *han* of people can be directly used as energy for social development should not be blindly accepted. It is a false belief originated from the void of schizoid *han*. Social movements based on human values and love can bring about reconciliation, trust, hope, and wholeness to the society.

CHAPTER V

THE *HAN* IN THE SYMBOLISM OF KOREAN SHAMANISM

Korean Shamanism is the oldest religion in Korea, its origin dating back to antiquity. It shares the same basic structure of the types of Shamanism that exist in the area of north-eastern Asia and Japan.[1] It also has some unique characteristics that distinguish it from other forms of Shamanism. For example, in Siberian Shamanism sacrifice is the central issue; in Japanese Shamanism ritualistic procedures for the dead are focused on; and in Korean Shamanism the climax is in playing with the gods through singing and dancing.[2] Beneath these phenomena lies the most important characteristic of Korean Shamanism, the symbolism of *han*. Korean Shamanism has developed around the central issue of *han* throughout its long history, and its main task has been to resolve or to prevent *han* on a personal as well as collective level.[3] "Sinbyung," which is common to shamans in Siberia and Japan, is understood in Korea in relation to *han*.[4]

Han is the basis of the psychological disturbances. It can also be more than just a pathological phenomenon that should be eradicated. Something positive is contained in it. The understanding of the symbolic

97

meaning of the practices of Korean Shamanism gives lights into this positive aspect.

In previous chapters, the focus of study was on the analysis of the nature of *han*. This approach is necessary for understanding the inner dynamics of the pathology, as well as the creativity of *han*, but alone is insufficient because understanding the root of *han* is not enough. "Freedom to" is as important as "freedom from" in the discussion of the meaning of *han*. A different approach, synthetic-constructive[5] than reductive-analytic, is needed to be helpful in delving into the meaning of *han* in this direction. Carl G. Jung provides a model for this type of approach that is invaluable in the exploration of the meaning of *han*.

Jung approaches the psyche symbolically. Because the psyche speaks in symbols, we must learn its language and the symbolic modes of communication. By symbol, Jung means "a nonrational, figurative constellation that points beyond itself to unknown or unknowable objective reality and makes that reality perceptible to us."[6] Because the psyche speaks in symbols, which communicate through analogies, it is natural for Jung to use analogies instead of analysis in order to communicate what the psyche speaks. By making an analogy based on something known, knowledge of something unknown is mediated. This approach therefore, takes the images seriously as something having their intrinsic, unique values. Jung's understanding of symbol is different from that of Freud. Freud sees the symbol as a disguise, a mask that can and must be removed (analyzed) to reveal what lies beneath it (the Oedipal complex). Jung sees the symbol not as a disguise, but as the best possible expression of an unknown or unknowable reality that is conveyed by the image. So, with Jung's synthetic-constructive method, we ask questions such as what does the symbol lead to, and lead us to see or grasp? Symbols should not be produced at will. They must be treated as the self-expression of the psyche itself. Also symptoms are treated not as a kind of signal for the problem to be corrected but as a kind of message carrying meaning, purpose, and direction for the future.[7]

1. The "Barikongjoo" Myth and *Han*

(1) The "Barikongjoo" Myth in Korean Shamanism.

The "Barikongjoo" myth is one of the few most important shaman myths among the more than one hundred of them, in terms of its popularity as well as its psychological and religious meanings. It is recited by the "mutang" (female shaman) at the "Chinogi kut" (a ritual for the recently dead soul), or at other shaman rituals that are performed for the stray spirits that are unable to enter the nether world because of the *han* resulting from their extremely unhappy deaths. The "Chinogi kut" belongs to the category of rituals for the spirits of the dead, which is one of the three main categories of shaman rituals. The other two are blessing rituals and healing rituals.[8] The function of the shaman in this ritual is to resolve the *han* of the dead spirit and lead the spirit safely to the nether world. Kwang-sun Suh describes the "weltanschaung" of Korean Shamanism as follows;

> When a person dies he or she dies only physically. The soul
> lingers around the body "observing" what the relatives are
> doing. The soul is not dead yet; that is, the soul has not
> departed to its proper place. A farewell kut is needed to help
> the soul to go to the place for the dead. Some dead are not
> ready to die; some die by accident and some die too young.
> But the death itself is something sad and unhappy and
> unpleasant. There is a lot of *han* in a death. Thus, the kut for
> the dead is to release the sad feeling, or *han*, which the dead
> person has accumulated during his life time. Even if the dead
> person led a happy life without any *han* (which is most
> unlikely), the death itself is a great *han* for him, and the
> person needs release from the *han* of death itself.[9]

By reciting the "Barikongjoo" myth the shaman convinces people that she is the one who is empowered to lead the dead soul to the nether world. The shaman becomes identified with "Barikongjoo," the heroine, as she recites the epic. The success of the ritual depends upon how well she can identify herself with "Barikongjoo" and tell the story as if it were her personal story. The *han* of the individual shaman is reactivated while she is performing the role of "Barikongjoo" in the ritual. At the same time the *han* of the participants are also reactivated and reexperienced. The reason the goddess of "Barikongjoo" is especially favored by shamans from amongst the many other deities in Korean Shamanism is that because her story reflects the *han* of the shamans themselves. It is a well held view among both scholars and the public that shamans are individuals who have suffered much *han*, and overcome it in the process of becoming shaman. By overcoming their *han* they acquire the power to heal the wounds of other people and become the priestess or the priest of *han*.[10] Because the story of "Barikongjoo" carries the prototype of the shaman's han, it is loved by the shamans as their own stories.

The psychological meaning of the "Barikongjoo" myth reveals the process of the transformation on *han*. The story, of course, does not directly tell us how *han* is transformed and into what. It tells only indirectly, through symbols that must be interpreted.

Dong-shik Ryu and Tae-gon Kim, following the guidelines of Mircea Eliade, interpret the "Barikongjoo" myth as the process of leaving the ordinary secular world and returning to the primordial mythical world. To where all the opposites between God and mortal and nature and human are resolved, and where exists the principle of nirvana.[11]

Kwang-il Kim interprets the "Barikongjoo" myth from the perspective of orthodox Freudian psychology as an expression of the Oedipus complex. He claims that Bari's neglect for her mother while reviving her father with medicine water reveals the hidden motive, which is the wish to marry her father and kill her mother.[12]

These interpretations, yet, do not give proper consideration to the symbolic meanings of the images and symbols in the epic of "Barikongjoo." It seems a significant task to render a psychological commentary on the myth while giving emphasis to the symbolic meanings of the images and symbols in the story.

(2) The Epic of "Barikongjoo"

In the early days, there was a king named "Ogu" who had no son, but several daughters. When the seventh daughter was born, he was greatly frustrated and put her in a stone box and cast it into a pond. Out of compassion, however, Heaven sent a dragon king to rescue the girl from the pond and to bring her to the mountain spirit to be cared for. This daughter, "Barikongjoo," lived happily in the mountain without knowing who she was, for any question she asked about her parents was not answered.

One day the king became critically ill. His wife learned that the only thing that could cure his illness was the medicine water in the western fountain. She asked the other six daughters, who grew up as princesses and were married to those of high rank in the nation, to go to the fountain, but all refused with different excuses. With the help of the mountain spirit who came to her in a dream, she could finally locate the deserted princess Bari in a deep mountain. Upon her request, Bari gladly returned to the palace with her mother.

"Barikongjoo," the rejected princess, volunteered to go to the place to get the medicine water. She disguised herself as a man and left on the journey. On her way she met first an old man with an ox, working in a huge field, who asked her to cultivate the whole field in return for directions. The work was too hard for her, and she became sad and began to weep helplessly. Then, with a sudden strong wind, thousands of moles appeared from the heavens and cultivated the field in a moment.

Next on her journey she met an old woman who was washing two huge piles of clothes by the stream. She wanted Bari to wash the clothes in return for her directions. Forgetting about the journey for a moment Bari decided to help the lady, not because of her need but out of sympathy toward the lady. The laundry was in two piles; one white and the other black. Bari had to wash the white clothes until they became black and the black until they became white. Besides the cold weather, the task was extremely difficult, for at first she could not make the white clothes black just by washing. She finally found, however, that the white clothes became black if she washed them in muddy water. After completing her task she removed all the lice in the hair of the old lady, who was taking a nap.

The third person she met on her journey was a young man, the keeper of the medicine water. He was assigned this job as punishment for a sin that he had committed in heaven. Only when he marries and has three sons will his sin be forgiven, and will he be allowed to ascend to heaven. He was waiting for the appearance of a woman who could save him from this predicament. When he discovered that Bari was a young woman, he asked her to marry him and to bear three sons in return for the directions. This she did and as promised, after she gave birth to the third son, he revealed the way to the source of the medicine water.

She traveled thousands of miles more to get to the fountain and finally arrived at the place. Inside a flower garden stood a stone pillar, and from the top of it, which was shaped like the head of a turtle, the medicine water was dripping. She filled a little turtle-shaped container and then sealed it with flowers of red, blue, yellow and white. On her journey back, she found that her husband returned to heaven leaving his three sons at home. With her three sons, she hurried back to her father's kingdom. On her way back to the world, she met many Buddhas who were coming toward her in the ship sent to help her safely cross the sea that separates this world from the nether world.

When she arrived, her father was already dead and was about to be buried, but the medicine water she brought revived him and restored him to health. She was offered the highest position in the royal court, but she refused and instead became the first ancestor of all mutangs. Her task was to lead stray souls into heaven.[13]

This story of "Barikongjoo" can be interpreted as a psychological and spiritual journey of the *han*-ridden women of Korea. The following is an attempt at its interpretation.

(3) The Original *Han* of "Barikongjoo"

The story of "Barikongjoo" is not about the nature of *han* itself, but about the process of the transformation of *han*. In Korean Shamanism, *han* is treated as something inseparable from the totality of one's life. This is why often the *han* of an individual is identified with the whole course of his or her life. In the broader sense of its meaning, then, the *han* of "Barikongjoo" includes the entire story of her journey, the whole process of transformation of *han*. Still, differentiation between original and secondary *han* is helpful to avoid unnecessary confusion and the inflation of the meaning of the word. The secondary *han* is produced by the accumulated frustrations and losses of love objects that are experienced throughout life. It can reactivate or intensify the original *han*, but it cannot replace it. The original *han* is entrenched in the deep layer of one's personality and is beyond the limits of one's conscious memory. It can be reactivated or intensified, but it resists modification by the secondary *han*.

In the story of "Barikongjoo" the original *han* took place right after her birth. Because she was born female her existence was rejected, and she was deserted by her parents. Without even receiving a name from her parents, she was called "Barikongjoo," which means deserted princess.[14] The word "Bari" is derived from the Korean verb "buhrida," which means "to desert." She was rejected by her parents, or more accurately by her father, as her mother was also a victim of the social norms and was unable to resist the king's order and save her baby.

This reflects the actual life experience of most women during the period of the Yi dynasty, in which, under the influence of Confucianism, women were the subject of oppression and contempt in the male dominant society.[15] The discrimination against females in that society was so extreme that the existence of femininity is often directly identified with *han*. In that environment, the feminine being takes negative than positive expression and is described symbolically as "ensnaring, fixating, holding fast, leading from light to darkness, depriving, rejecting, acting as a regressive undertow of unconsciousness that drags one beyond one's depth, to be swallowed up."[16] In reality, it might have been a rare occasion when a baby girl was deserted by her parents. But what most young women experienced in their infantile minds was no less painful than actual desertion. We could imagine that they found in the eyes of their mothers, not pride in the spontaneous gestures of their daughters, but instead disappointment and contempt. The girl babies introject these feelings into the core of their beings.

This process can be explained with the idea of the basic psychological mechanisms of projection and introjection. In the interaction between mother and baby, the mother projects the contents of her unconscious onto the baby, while the baby introjects what is projected onto it. The mother's unconscious contempt for her baby girl is partly what she inherited from her mother when she was a little baby, and partly what she absorbed from social norms. The contempt transmitted from the mother is also the product of society, for if the society is based on a belief in female inferiority, the females in the society are liable to form an unconscious belief of their inferiority. This belief must be kept in the unconscious, away from conscious awareness, because it is too painful an idea to accept consciously, or it may be filed away as a part of the wisdom needed to survive in a male dominated society. When the mother sees her female baby, her feelings of inferiority that were repressed in her unconscious are invoked. She then splits off this feeling and projects it onto the baby as a defensive measure out of her weakness. This process takes place unconsciously without being noticed by others or even by the mother herself, and it becomes a source of sickness. As the Swiss psychoanalyst Alice Miller points out, "Things that we can see through do not make us sick, they arouse our indignation, anger, sadness, or feelings of impotence. What makes us sick are those things we cannot see through, society's constraints that we have absorbed through our mother's eyes."[17] In the story of "Barikongjoo," though the king did not even see the baby girl, she experienced the king's rejection through the eyes of her mother who was forced to obey his orders and abandon the baby.

It is a common folk belief in Korea that the *han* of women is deeper than that of men. This belief is supported in that women form the mainstream of Korean Shamanism, the religion of *han*. It is more than a coincidence to find that most shamans recall that, from the time they were born, they were unwanted or disappointed children just because of their gender.[18] The *han* of the shaman represents the han of Korean women.[19]

The baby Bari was put into a stone box and cast into the pond. This can be taken as the symbolic expression of the withdrawal of the baby's ego from reality and hiding within. She shut herself off from the object relationship and withdrew into the stone box, hidden in the pond of the unconscious. Withdrawal is the natural reaction of the baby's ego when it finds itself in an unwelcome environment. When a baby encounters rejection very early, she is liable to hide the split off, original part of herself.

The beginnings of original *han* may go back further to existential human nature itself, similar to the idea of original sin which St. Augustine explicates in his theological work. Both suggest the mysterious roots of negative forces arising in our instinctual level of psyche. Original *han* in Korean minds, however, concerns more on the experiential phenomena than on the pre-experiential and existential principle of human nature. Original *han* draws our attention to the conflicting positive and negative forces operative in ourselves, as does original sin. The difference between original *han* and original sin lies on the level of the ego's capacity to recognize the psychic reality. The awareness of original sin requires a minimum level of psychic maturity to be able to recognize it without totally blaming others, whereas original *han* belongs to a more archaic level of psyche, incapable of recognizing reality, blaming others totally. Original sin is an idea opposite to original goodness, which presupposes a psychic state in which the process of splitting between good and bad has already taken place; in contrast, original *han* is an idea that has no opposite.

(4) The Symbolic Meaning of Bari's Journey
Under the care of the mountain spirit, "Barikongjoo" had a happy childhood without experiencing many of life's hardships. This was a period of latency, during which she could maintain her inner peace in a state of repression. Her quest for identity was repressed until, with the onset of adolescence. At the age of fourteen, she was reunited with her parents and returned home, where a great challenge awaited her. She was to go to the western fountain (or "hwangchun") to seek the medicine water needed to heal her father (in some versions of the story, both

parents). A journey to the western fountain means a journey to the world of the dead. In the language of depth psychology, especially that of analytical psychology, it means the journey to the realm of the unconscious. This journey and the return is equivalent to the "individuation" process discussed by Carl G. Jung.[20]

The goal of Bari's journey is to find the medicine water and return with it to her father's kingdom. In some other versions, a heavenly herb is required instead of medicine water. Both are panaceas that can cure any disease and even revive the dead, and they can be found only after long, painful journey in search of them.

To start this journey, great courage is needed to break off all ties and leave behind the safety of this world. The other six sisters refused to take the risk for various reasons. Only Bari, who had *han* because of being deserted by her parents, decided to start the journey. She sings out:

> Seven princesses were called out for sacrifice to save the lives of father and mother. Though I received no favor from the country and the court I was given life for ten months in the womb of my mother. To save my parents' life I will go.[21]

Bari decided to volunteer to help her parents because of her gratitude for their giving life to her. She had a basic trust in the goodness of life, the basis from which she could start a journey of life. A wish to make reparation is showed in the song of Bari's departure. We could imagine that Bari psychologically reached the stage where she could perceive "the damaged objects" in her self and could feel sorry about that. To restore the critically ill parents she decided to go on the journey.

A. Father Complex

According to Jung's discovery, the process of individuation begins with dealing with the contents of the unconscious, which he called complex. Jung explains that "a complex is an emotionally charged unconscious psychic entity made up a number of associated ideas and images clustered around a central core . . . [which is] an archetypal image."[22] The complex consists emotionally charged images, conditioned by childhood situations and personal history.[23] At the core of every complex is a transpersonal, universal human pattern of experience, symbolized in archetypal images. The task involved in the course of the individuation process is to resolve the shell part of the complex through integrating it with the self so that the core part of it has the opportunity to unfold and bloom to its potential.

The psychic entity of the complex refers to the reality of *han*. *Han* can be viewed as "a network of emotionally charged images" conditioned by childhood situations and personal history. On the negative side, *han* is responsible for the creation of unduly intense aggression and fearful images that cause difficulty in one's emotional and social life. It consists of feelings of inferiority, rejected wishes, and frustrations. On the positive side, *han* contains the potential of one's true life, protected by the shell part. Jung calls this potential the archetypes that express themselves through images. The archetypal images are charged with powerful energies that can be channeled into both negative or positive usages. The same archetypal images express themselves in symbols of *han* whose images are more often in negative forms of bad and fearful objects. It shows the distorted, exaggerated, and fragmented images of the archetypes. *Han*, yet, can be healed or transformed into the energy for creativity and expresses the genuine, proportionate, and whole picture of archetypes. The process of the healing of *han* parallels the process of the transformation of the images of *han*. The process of individuation parallels the process of the emergence of the true archetypal images of *han*, and our relating to them appropriately. Therefore, *han* is not simply something to be gotten rid of. It contains not only the negative side but also the positive side. The negative complex should be resolved, but the resolution of the complex is not the goal. It is a needed step in the process of achieving the true goal of life; the actualization of the true self in relation to archetypal images.

The first figure Bari meets on her journey is an old man who gives her the task of cultivating a large field with an ox. The wise man who often appears as a mountain spirit in Korean fairy tales represents the principle of the wisdom that comes from the unconscious. During her journey Bari gets help from the old man when she does not know which way to turn. According to Edward Edinger, a noted American Jungian analyst, the figure of the wise old man is also a representation of the father archetype. On the collective level, the father archetype represents the principle of spirit, reason, and wisdom. The archetype of the spiritual father represents the masculine as the principle of consciousness symbolized by light, spirit, the sun, the heavens, and the wind. Its function is to convey law, order, discipline, rationality, understanding and inspiration. For Bari, the mountain spirit is the image of a positive father that balances the negative father who rejected her. In the story her father rejected her and tried to kill her, which is a clear example of a negative father complex. The father is felt to be the source of negative energy that leads to alienation from concrete reality. The figure of the old man in our story, who is depicted as weak and insensitive, demands she do work beyond her strength. He represents the negative father complex from which she must redeem the positive energies. Bari's first task is to deal with her father complex and assimilate the contents of it into her conscious ego. This was symbolized by the task of cultivating the barren field. The large field in the story symbolizes an individual's unconscious. The symbolic meaning of the cultivation of the field is the assimilation of one's unconscious complex into one's conscious ego.

Bari tried to cultivate the field, yet the job was too difficult for her. The ground was too hard to be penetrated, and the ox was so rough that instead of controlling the animal, she was being dragged by it. The ox represents the obstinacy of her father complex which sometimes possesses the ego with its power. It shows the uncontrollable character of the forces of a complex given conscious effort alone. As Jung points out, "everyone knows nowadays that people 'have complexes.' What is not so well known, though far more important theoretically, is that complexes can have us."[24]

The unconscious cannot be completely controlled by conscious effort alone, just as Bari could not handle the ox despite her conscious efforts. As Jung puts it:

> Without the cooperation of the unconscious and its instinctive
> forces, the conscious personality would be too weak to wrench

itself free from its infantile past, and venture into a strange world with all its unforeseen possibilities. The whole of the libido is needed for the battle of life.[25]

In the story of Bari, help came to her from the unconscious when she gave up the control of the ox and sat crying in the middle of the field. Then, with a sudden strong wind, a multitude of moles appeared and cultivated the field for her. Wind represents the spiritual principle emanating from the father archetype that gave Bari not only the task but also the energy to accomplish it. The mountain spirit, preserved in the Bari's deep psyche, seems to respond to her feelings and helplessness after she tried and failed to do the task. The mountain spirit stirs up the unconscious energies that are represented as blind moles.[26] The moles represent the elements of her self that were neglected, and deserted as something useless and a nuisance. They represent an instinctive and blind level of psychic life, an unconscious way of both digging up and ordering. They also might represent energies that when freed from the negative father complex can help uproot it, dig tunnels through it, loosen its soil. Her expression of feeling and her ego, so to speak, trying its best and reaching its limits, is rescued by the archetypal energy of the mountain spirit. Thus she can assimilate her complex that was stubborn like an ox and hard as the hardened soil. By the help of the very instinctual energies that have been held in contempt and repressed in the unconscious, the negative aspect of her father archetype was transformed into the positive aspect of the spiritual principle.

The ox is an animal figure that appears often in oriental fairy tales. In the tradition of Zen Buddhism, the ox is an animal that represent the mind of a person. In the beginning of the Zen story, a black ox usually appears, then a white spot forms on its skin and extends gradually until the ox becomes totally white. Dong-sik Lee interprets that the black ox represents the contents of the negative, self-destructive emotions in one's unconscious. Through the process of maturation of the personality the negative self-destructive emotions can be transformed into the constructive emotion of love.[27]

B. Mother Complex

The next figure Bari meets on her journey is an old woman. If the old man she met first was an archetypal figure of the father, the old woman is an archetypal figure of the mother. They are parental figures, not the personal, actual parents. Both can be of great help and are indispensable to the progress of her journey. Her task is to resolve the complex clustered around these figures and to liberate the archetypes from the complex. The archetypes entangled within the complex become negative and the source of problems that cause suffering in her life. In contrast, when they are freed from the complex (from the han), they become the sources of life energy--wisdom, growth and creativity.

It is important to note in the story that the images which represent Bari's unconscious complex are manifested in human form. In the first part of the story, images such as the dragon, mountain spirit, and ox are shown frequently. Later they are replaced by images in human form such as an old man, an old woman, and a young man. As Marie-Louise von Franz, a follower of Carl Jung, suggests, the manifestation of an archetype in a human form would demonstrate the possibility of conscious relation, whereas an inhuman form, or a natural power form would show the difficulty of conscious relation. The appearance of images in human form signifies a different stage in the individuation process from that of animal or supernatural forms of images.[28]

In some other versions of the "Barikongjoo" story, the old woman is called "mago-halmae," "malgo-hamuni," or "magoo-halmum,"[29] all of which are derived from the name of the legendary giant witch. These names are phonetically similar to the word "magui-halmum," which means an old witch. The description of her features in all versions of the story is very much like a witch figure, who looked ugly and dirty with her dirty hair and clothes infested with lice.

Bari dealt compassionately with this figure, saying, "Old lady, how cold you must be, washing all these clothes in the icy water in this cold weather! I will wash them for you."[30] A big change in her attitude is revealed in her warm, human feeling toward the old woman. Previously, she did not show such feelings when she met the old man. This time, she decided to do the task, not because she wanted information, but because of her compassion for the old lady. This change reveals the transformation that had already taken place within Bari's psyche. With the power of compassion, she could relate the two split images of her mother, the witch, and the loving mother. Also she could accept the rejected and despised aspect of herself, which was projected onto the image of an old woman. Now she could personally forgive the mother who deserted her when she was an infant.

Bari could not resist removing the lice from the old lady's hair and clothing even after she had finished her task of doing the laundry. This is a very powerful image of goodness overcoming badness. The old lady could sleep comfortably because of Bari's extra service and became happy when she woke up from her deep sleep. A loving mother-daughter relationship was established between her and the old lady, her mother figure. This feature of the story can be interpreted as the restoration of the mother as the primary object in her inner world. Bari's previous relation to her mother was based more on a sense of moral duty and necessity than on the feeling of unconditional, spontaneous love. Now her present relation to her mother figure is based on unconditional and spontaneous love. As Jung emphasizes, however, this kind of experience should not be interpreted only in relation to her real mother. Her journey "leads back only apparently to the mother; in reality she is the gateway into the unconscious, into the realm of the Mothers. It does not stop short at the 'mother' but goes back beyond her to the prenatal realm of the 'Eternal Feminine,' to the immemorial world of archetypal possibilities."[31] Eun Ko's case provides an example of this. By restoring his mother he eventually restores the Mother of all, the "Bodhi-Sattva," the representation of the mother archetype in Jung's language.[32] On the functions and attributes of the archetype of the Great Mother, Edward F. Edinger provides a succinct description.

> It is like the fertile womb out of which all life comes and the darkness of the grave to which it returns. Its fundamental attributes are the capacity to nourish and the capacity to devour. It corresponds to mother nature in the primordial swamp-like being constantly spawned and constantly devoured. If the great mother nourishes us, she is good; if she

threatens to devour us, she is bad. In psychological terms, the
great mother corresponds to theunconscious which can nourish
and support the ego or can swallow it up in psychosis or
suicide.[33]

What happened to Bari was not just a change in her personal relation
to her mother but was also a change in the constellation of the mother
archetype within her unconscious. Previously it had been entangled with
negative feelings and images resulting from her personal experiences of
her mother and had become a complex exerting negative influences on
her self. Now with the liberation of the mother archetype from the
negative mother-complex she can freely use the energy and feelings of
love flowing through the channel of the archetypal image of the mother.
This transformation is not earned easily, but a great achievement,
achieved only after the hard work of self-discipline.

Bari's task was to wash the two piles of clothes, the black and the
white, until the white turned black and the black turned white. One way
to understand this task psychologically is to view it as a process of
overcoming the polarity of the opposites by integrating the split parts of
the mind into one's consciousness. This is different from the confusion
that would result from mingling those parts together indiscriminately.
Instead, they had to be carefully sorted out into white wash and black
wash without mixing them together. Then the black laundry could be
washed in clean water until it becomes white, and the white laundry
should be washed in muddy water to make it black. This was not an
easy job. Strenuous work with conflicting ideas and feelings was
required in order for the ego to assimilate and bridge the split.

In other versions of the story, the task is to build a bridge over a
deep stream flowing through the gap between two cliffs. In essence,
building the bridge over the gap represents the same task of integration
of the split parts of the self. This split is located in the area between
conscious and unconscious, good mother and bad mother, and love and
hate. The white laundry represents the conscious aspect of one's psyche,
whereas the black laundry represents the unconscious aspect. The
process of making unconscious material conscious is symbolized by the
washing of the black laundry in the clean water. The conscious material

is mixed with the unconscious material that is represented by the mud and the muddy water. The strenuous activity of doing laundry represents the process of assimilation of the unconscious into the conscious ego. Bari's active participation, involving both her conscious and unconscious is needed at this stage, to proceed in the process of individuation.

The images of black laundry, mud, and muddy water can be regarded as the symbols for the contents of the personal *han*, which is composed of the repressed thoughts and feelings of an individual. It is analogous to Freud's idea of the unconscious as made up of the infantile mental life, repressed contents and unused sexual libido. In the narrow sense of its meaning, *han* is equivalent to the personal unconscious. However, *han* is more than the contents of the personal unconscious, for it contains an archetypal core. Without the archetypal core, the *han* will become a mere shell or shadow which is only negative. In fact, these become the formidable negative forces disturbing the psychic balance of an individual, because they are related to the archetypal images, the source of energy. Disturbance occurs when the contents of the psyche are split from the conscious ego and are repressed, becoming entangled with negative forces also existing in the unconscious to form a negative complex. The task here is to overcome this split by integrating the repressed contents of the personal unconscious into the conscious ego so that the archetypal image is restored to its original healthy functions. The *han* in the story of Bari shows that it is in the process of transformation that negative energy is transformed into creative life force.

C. Shadow

The shadow is the image used by Carl Jung to describe those mysterious, negative contents of both the personal and collective unconscious. It is a complex, its shell part has the repressed material on personal level, and is often personified as the evil. At the core of the shadow complex is the archetype, that is, an archetypal image of evil, like a devil or witch. The old woman in the story can be viewed as the personification of the shadow of Bari, also the image of her mother-complex. On the individual level, shadow is always represented by someone of the same sex one dislikes, or finds irritating or even hateful. When enough attention and care is given to this figure that represents those neglected aspects of ourselves, it becomes less threatening and more and more helpful to us.[34] On the individual level, our egos can work to integrate these split off parts of ourselves. To some extent, groups can try to do this on the collective level. But on the archetypal level the ego cannot assimilate evil per se. That would cause an ego-inflation or an ego-deflation. At this level the ego as well as the group must try to relate to evil, take measures to protect the self and the group, and carefully observe the ways of the evil powers. The shadow can develop either way. "Toward the daimonic, the advocate who pleads for a larger perspective, pushing us to go beyond our narrowness, to find courage to create our unique being-in-the-world, or it can move toward the negative pole, as an antagonist leading us into a malevolent darkness that destroys meaning."[35] It should be noted that in the story the old woman is identified with a witch figure who, when well treated with care and love, turns out to be a good witch, which provides Bari with the needed information for her further journey. A shadow figure can also be negative and drag us beyond the level of personal material to a level of archetypal evil.

D. Animus

The anima and animus are symbolic concepts that Jung uses to describe the psychic function that mediates between the objective and personal unconscious. The anima in the man's psyche and the animus in the woman's have the function of mediating between the ego and this objective psyche. These terms do not refer to figures that exist as physical entities, but instead refer to clusters of psychic energy around an archetypal core which act as if they were secondary contrasexual personalities. To proceed in the individuation process Bari has to claim her femaleness, relate to it, and join with it in marriage to the animus. This part of the drama shows that the next stage of the individuation process is to deal with the image of one's contrasexuality and to integrate it through the symbolic act of marriage. This stage does not belong to the realm of only the personal unconscious any more, but also to the realm of the collective unconscious or objective psyche.[36] The objective psyche refers to a deeper layer of the unconscious which, unlike the personal unconscious, is ordinarily inaccessible to consciousness. The objective psyche is nonindividual, universal, and suprapersonal. Jung describes; "The opposite sex is human, hence we can communicate with it, but it speaks and moves and acts from a totally other frame of reference."[37]

The young man in the story represents the animus figure for Bari, and her task is to integrate the contents of her objective psyche into her conscious ego. This is done by marriage, which symbolizes the uniting of the sexual polarities of feminine and masculine. She has to get in the right relation with the feminine and masculine parts of herself. Meanwhile, her animus was waiting for her like Sleeping Beauty awaiting the arrival of the prince. When Bari arrives in the disguise of a man, the young man takes all kinds of initiatives and is assertive in discovering her true sexuality and in persuading her to marry him. He is the personification of the qualities that Bari desperately needed to achieve the goal of her journey, and without which she could not have penetrated to the exact location of the medicine water. These qualities of the animus archetype are succinctly summarized by Ann Ulanov;

> As a pattern of behavior, the animus archetype represents instinctive drive behavior related to the masculine as symbolizing an elemental dynamism of life. The masculine symbolizes those drive elements related to active initiative, to aggressive assertiveness, to the search for meaning, to creativity, and to one's capacity for discrimination, separation, and judgement. As a pattern of emotion, the animus consists of woman's unconscious capacity to focus on, evaluate, and discern her own reactions, her unconscious rationality, her power aspirations, her opinions, her argumentativeness, her aggression, her capacities to differentiate, her expectations of how one "ought to be" and "what one should do," as well as her potential for relationship to creative meaning, clarity, self-expression, and the spiritual contents of her life.[38]

On a deeper level of Bari's *han* exists a split between the feminine and masculine elements in her psyche. The masculine element, which is symbolized in the image of a young man, is condemned, isolated, and repressed. In the story the young man was condemned because he did "what he should not." This can mean that Bari's self-assertiveness was rejected by the social norm and thus withdrawn into the deep area of the unconscious. She needs in this stage to liberate the masculine aspect of her sexuality and integrate it in her total personality in order to utilize its energy when necessary. For Bari this means to learn to be assertive or aggressive based on love.

E. Persona

Bari disguised herself as man to hide her sexual identity and to protect herself from the dangers of external reality, but before long her identity was exposed to the young man. The image of clothes represents the mask whose function is to defend the identity and to adjust to the external reality. Jung uses the symbolic concept persona (actor's mask) to refer to the psychic function, which mediates between the ego and the external world. It is as if the psyche develops a social role and assumes a public face when adapting to others.[39] The persona mediates between one's own individuality and the expectations of society. It tells one what role is appropriate in public situations and protects what is personal and private. Bari's removal of the disguise means that in the course of the individuation process she had to learn to differentiate her persona from her identity. This does not mean she had to throw away her social masks and become naked, but it does mean that her role should be flexible enough that it can be taken up and put aside at will. For her this was a prerequisite to entering into the relationship with her animus.

F. The Self

After giving birth to her third son, Bari was informed about the secret way to reach the place of the medicine water. Leaving the children under the care of the husband, she left for that place, and, after passing narrow and dangerous passages through the valleys and rocky mountains, she finally arrived at the medicine water fountain. There she found a garden of beautiful flowers, in which stood a huge and robust stone piercing through the sky. The top part of the stone pillar was shaped like the head of a turtle from which the medicine water was dripping down. She picked up a small bottle shaped like a turtle, filled it with the water of life, and sealed it with a flower.[40]

The stone from which the water of life flows is in the image of a phallus symbolizing masculine sexuality, and the bottle receiving the dripping water from the phallus is like the image of the vagina, symbolizing feminine sexuality. The top part of the phallus is called "gui-doo," which literally means a turtle head. The image of turtle can be more than a symbol of sexuality. Its rounded shell on top symbolizes heaven and the square underneath represents earth. Heaven is a symbol of spiritual reality whereas earth is of material existence. Its slowness means natural evolution and longevity.[41] As a whole, these images depict a picture of a "*hieros gamos*," which is the symbolic expression of the "*coniunctio oppositorum*." In the teachings of oriental philosophy, the unity of the opposite sexes of feminine and masculine represents the wholeness of a person, which is the goal of self-discipline. The symbol of wholeness is often expressed in the image of "Tae Geuk (or Yin and Yang)," a mandala image.[42]

These features of the fountain show the archetype of the self, which is the central archetype expressing psychic wholeness, order and totality. It is not only the center but also the whole circumference that embraces both the conscious and the unconscious. It contains a paradoxical unity encompassing all the polarities of the psyche that are symbolized most often in terms of the masculine-feminine polarity. As Ulanov puts it, "The wholeness of the self is built up from the reconciliation of these opposite psychic poles, but not from their fusion, because the tension of the opposites remains the source of life's energy and the dynamism of the self."[43]

The self is often represented in myths or fairy tales by such symbols as the "Yu Eu Joo" (pearl in the mouth of the dragon), the medicine herb, medicine water, or bottled medicine water. It is also represented by the mandala in its varied forms, such as "Tae Geuk," the lotus, and the circle in the square, etc.. It is sometimes represented in human forms such as the divine image of Buddha or Christ.[44]

The image of the bottled water sealed with flowers in our story also represents a symbol of the self. This image is very close to the image of the sealed retort topped with a peacock displaying its tail, which Marie-Louise von Franz illustrates as the symbol of the self. The peacock, symbolizing the renewal of life, rises from the sealed retort in which takes place the union of opposites, integration of masculine and feminine.[45] In our story the image of flowers, instead of the peacock, symbolizes the renewal of life. Those flowers of the colors red, blue, yellow, and white, according to other versions of the story, represent the revival of certain parts of the body, blood, bone, flesh, and breath.

The images of the Buddhas Bari meets on her way back to this world are also the symbols of the archetype of the self.[46] The image of a ship floating on the sea of death, containing six Buddhas, can be viewed as a picture of mandala. This is the mandala that appears after a long period of psychological and spiritual development, which also symbolizes the transformation of *han*.

G. Vocation

The theme of the renewal of life takes concrete form when Bari, returning to the human world, opens the casket and revives her dead father with the medicine water.[47] A big feast follows to celebrate the occasion. This scene may look like the climax of the story, but seen from the perspective of the individuation process, the climax of the story is found not as much in the celebration as in its simple end of the story. Finally, when Bari was offered by the revived king a high position in court with many luxuries, she refused them. Instead, she volunteered to become a shaman to lead stray souls to the other world.

At the culmination of the individuation process Bari finds her vocation, which is distinguished from the conventional way of life. Her destiny was to resolve the *han* of the souls of both the dead and the living. In Korean Shamanism it is believed that dead souls go astray because of their *han*. The shaman is the administrator of *han* who tries to resolve the *han* of the stray soul and lead it to the nether world. The psychological meaning of the shaman's role is the creation of a new person by transforming the negative *han* into creative energy, analogous to the process of an alchemist creating gold from base metal. The shaman is a person who has gone through this process. Bari's experiences on her journey represent the process of the transformation of the shaman's *han* as well as the process of the birth of a new person. The newly emerged person who arises out of the old person of *han* is the person of vocation, described by Jung:

> It is what is commonly called vocation; an irrational factor that destines a man to emancipate himself from the herd and from its well-worn paths. True personality is always a vocation and puts its trust in it as in God, despite its being, as the ordinary man would say, only a personal feeling. But vocation acts like a law of God from which there is no escape. The fact that many a man who goes his own way ends in ruin means nothing to one who has a vocation. He must obey his own law, as if it were a daemon whispering to him of new and wonderful paths. Anyone with a vocation hears the voice of the inner man; he is called.[48]

The acceptance of vocation marks the stage of maturity in one's personality development. The whole process of personality development can be viewed as a journey to find one's vocation. Bari's journey was just such a journey. A shaman is one whose vocation has been found and accepted after a long process of personality development. Most Korean shamans find their vocation through "sinbyung," mental or psycho-somatic illnesses ranging from neurosis to psychosis. What they find in "sinbyung" is that they are destined to become shamans, and unless they accept their destiny they will never be healed. The longer they resist their vocation, the longer they suffer. "Sinbyung" is thus a defense against the inner calling of the psyche, or an attempt, somewhat dearly paid for, to escape from the inner calling of vocation. Jung points out that "behind the neurotic perversion is concealed his vocation, his destiny; the growth of personality, the full realization of the life-will that is born with the individual. It is the man without *amor fati* who is the neurotic."[49] This insight can be applied to the relationship between the han and vocation. The meaning of han is to become the person whose vocation is to serve God and man. Behind the symptom of han is concealed one's vocation, one's destiny; the growth of personality, the full realization of life. It is the woman or man without *amor fati* who becomes the person of *han*.

The "calling" that shamans experience is the invitation to lead stray soul to the "hwang-chun," the fountain of life, across the sea of the unconscious. The stray soul, in Jungian perspective, refers to the inner state of a person who is entangled by the forces of unconscious complexes (or *han*). There are various complexes that shackle souls to states of confusion, ignorance, and conflict, such as the mother complex, the father complex, the anima/animus complex, etc.. The soul has to be liberated from these complexes to reach the "suh-chun," the western fountain. The core part of the complex is the archetype and is the source of the energy of life, which has to be protected by the shell part of it. The positive function of the shell of the complex is to protect the core from external dangers while the ego tries to adjust to external reality. The shell part can become the source of negative forces, if it is too rigid and impenetrable by the life energy. The archetype is imprisoned by this type of shell. Then it negatively influences the quality of the energy flowing from the archetype.

This does not mean that archetypal energies are always positive. The archetype has in it both negative and positive potentiality. So it is not just the shell part that makes the core archetype negative. Sometimes the root of negative energy originates from the impersonal archetypal dimension. Despite the existence of negative energy that stems from archetype itself and is independent from the shell part of the complex, the importance of the influence of the shell over the ego's relationship with the archetype should not be underestimated. When the archetype is liberated from the grip of the shell of the complex, consisting of negative feelings, thoughts, and images accumulated through the personal experience of life, it can be transformed into a great helper, the provider of wisdom, energy and love necessary for further growth. At the least its positive potential becomes more accessible.

The shell part of the complex is equivalent to the psychic reality of *han* in its narrow meaning. Because the core of the complex, the archetype, is hidden deep in one's unconscious, the complex is often considered as only the negative contents of the psyche. In the same way *han* is easily considered as only the negative forces of the psyche because the core part is hidden, surrounded by the shell. Inside the shell exists the core of *han*, both positive and negative. Those who see this core part of *han* and are fascinated by it may easily idealize the phenomena of *han*, and forget its negative aspect. The negative aspect of the core of *han* should never be underestimated, for it may "lure us beyond the level of personal material to a level of archetypal evil that seems to be so impersonal and unalterably opposed to human consciousness that we can react only with horror."[50] Thus the core part of han should be dealt with, with the utmost care and caution in order to be used as positive energy by the conscious ego.

This work of integration is symbolized in the epic of Bari by the tasks of cultivating the field, laundering the clothes, marriage with the young man, and acceptance of the vocation. The sequence of her tasks reveals an increase of self-consciousness about the deeper layer of her complexes. Through this process takes place the healing of the *han* and the development of the personality. "Suh-chun" is a representation of the archetype of the self whence flows the water of life. To lead the stray soul to "suh-chun" essentially means to help people of *han* reach their archetypes of the self through the process of individuation. The calling of the shaman is the calling for a fuller life, for a wider and deeper understanding, and for the healing of the *han* of suffering people.

2. The Rituals of Korean Shamanism & *Han*

(1) The Basic Structure of the Ritual of Korean Shamanism

Though there are many different kinds of shaman rituals in Korea, their basic structure is essentially the same. The ritual consists of three steps: an invitation to the gods to descend, playing with the gods through song and dance, and a postlude.[51]

A. "Chungshin" (Invocation)

As the first step, the shaman in prayer invites the gods and spirits to the ritual. The descent of the gods is actualized when she goes into a trance. Singing and dancing, accompanied by music, are indispensable in this process. The shaman in a trance becomes the medium for gods and spirits and takes on multiple roles of different spirits according to the particular situation of the ritual.

B. "Ohshin" (Entertaining the Gods)

After the shaman enters the trance state, she begins to entertain the gods. Three elements are included in this part; communication, negotiation, and entertainment. The shaman relays the message of the gods to the participants. The messages of the gods are usually from the spirit of an ancestor summoned in the shaman's trance. A dialogue follows between the ancestor spirit and the family. The shaman and the family talk back and forth about the situation. This phenomenon can be understood as a dialogue between the conscious and the unconscious.

The spirit of the ancestor is the projected image of the unconscious complex of the family member. What actually dealt with in this process is not the *han* of the spirits of the dead but the *han* of the living. While in the state of trance, the shaman can speak from the unconscious side of the living person and translate the contents of the unconscious into a symbolic language that makes possible communication between the conscious and the unconscious. Negotiation is the process of realistic adjustment between the demands of the unconscious and those of the conscious within the limitations of reality. During the ritual, the ancestors and the spirits ask for more money, and food and drink, in return for their blessing. Then the members of the family negotiate with them to reach a mutually agreeable point. Food and drinks are shared by the participants. Money usually goes to the shaman or her group. Finally, there is a festive reconciliation when the blessings of the gods and spirits are proclaimed by the shaman, and joy is expressed in her singing and dancing. People are invited to dance together with the gods. This is a lively session, with song and dance, costume changes, tears,

shouts, jokes and laughter.[52] This part of the ritual symbolizes the
process of the reconciliation between the conscious and the unconscious.
"Heung" (excitement) or "sinmyung" (ecstatic joy) is the most prominent
element in this stage. Some even conclude that "heung" or "sinmyung"
is the element that brings about the resolution of *han*. Heu-wan Chae in
his study of shaman dance asserts that the "sinmyung" in the dances
resolves the *han* of the people[53], whereas Yul-kyu Kim acknowledges
three elements that bring the resolution of *han*: solemnity, pathos, and
joy. Kim views that when these three elements of shaman ritual interact
with each other and create an intensified "sinmyung," this "sinmyung"
brings forth the effect of healing.[54] The idea that "sinmyung" is the cure
of the *han* is most clearly seen in Hun-young Im's diagram in which he
schematized "sinmyung" as the turning point from *han*.

> *Han* -- wonhan -- revengeful emotion -- sinmyung experience
> -- social consciousness -- revolution.
>
> *Han* -- jeong-han -- emotion of resignation -- sinmyung
> experience -- adjustment to the reality -- national nihilism.[55]

The view that "sinmyung" resolves *han* is, yet, based on a simplistic
interpretation of the isolated phenomenon of the ritual process.
"Sinmyung" is not something that can be evoked by the magical power
of the shaman or simply by the effect of music and dancing. "Sinmyung"
should be understood as the result of the resolution of *han* than as the
cause of the resolution of *han*. It is an element that facilitates the process
of healing, but to reach this stage of ecstatic joy, one must go through
the processes of working through his complexes. "Sinmyung" comes
only after the resolution of *han* or, at least, with a partial resolution of
han. It is the result of reconciliation. The "sinmyung" itself has some
therapeutic effect, but, as Yul-kyu Kim discerns, its effect depends upon
interaction with other elements of the ritual such as solemnity and
pathos. The experience of solemnity and pathos, which is the nadir of
the ritual, is indispensable for arriving at the peak experience of
"sinmyung." The reexperiencing of *han* and its suffering in the ritual,
through the processes of communication and negotiation with the

contents of *han* reactivated by the shaman, is an integral part of the resolution of *han*.

C. "Songshin" (Bidding the Gods Farewell)

The third and final stage in the ritual is to praise the spirits or ancestors and bid farewell to them. If the ritual is for the stray souls of the dead, in this stage they are led to the other world by the shaman who, while singing and dancing, cuts through the middle of some twenty feet of white cloth with scissors. This part of the ritual is called "gilgarem," which literally means "opening the way." The cloth symbolizes the bridge between this world and the other world, which is opened for the stray souls to cross with the guidance of the shaman. This ritual is called "Chinogi-kut," which means the ritual for calming the soul gone astray, or "Dari-kut," which means the bridge ritual. The ritual action of cutting symbolizes the liberation of the soul from the *han*. The liberated soul now belongs to its proper place, which is the other world. In "Chunla" province (southern-west part of Korea), a different symbol is used for the liberation of the soul from the *han*. In that area the *han* is symbolized as seven knots on a long white cotton cloth. These are unknotted one by one by the shaman while singing and dancing.[56] As the knots representing deep wounds in the mind are unknotted one by one, the wounds themselves are gradually healed, and the wounded soul becomes whole again, and strong enough to start the journey to "hwangchun," the source of life. Bou-yong Rhie suggests that, what is actually dealt with in this ritual are the contents of the individual's unconscious. Personal complexes are reactivated and re-experienced to be used as new materials for a new personality. He describes;

> A death of a close person always takes away a portion of one's conscious personality. The degree of the feeling of the loss depends upon the degree of identification between the dead and the living. The split part of the ego remains in the unconscious and forms a powerful complex. In folk belief this is considered as the soul of the dead. The purpose of the mourning process for the dead is to bring the unconscious

contents into the conscious. The ritual for the dead is a system
to resolve the *han* of the living people.[57]

The function of the shaman is more than just to resolve the *han* of
the living, but also to lead the soul to "hwangchun." The goal of life,
the "hwangchun" is, in Jung's language, the world of archetypes. In this
sense, it can be said that the shaman is the facilitator of the individuation
process. It is unclear to what degree shamans are consciously aware of
their function as the facilitators of the individuation process of the
living, than the resolvers of the *han* of the spirits of the dead. Despite
the scarcity of research in this area, the shamans seem to be aware of
the transformation process of the personality. The self-consciousness of
the shaman is clearly expressed in the symbolism of "naerim-kut," the
initiation ritual.

(2) The Symbolism of Initiation Ritual and *han*
The "Hwanghae-do (northern-west province of Korea) nearim-kut
(initiation ritual) consists of eighteen rituals, and takes three days to
complete.[58] Among them, three are crucial; "huten-kut" (the false spirits
ritual), "naerim-kut" (the initiation ritual), "sosle-kut" (the emergence
ritual). In recent practice of Korean Shamanism, only these three are
performed for the initiation instead of the full eighteen.[59] Each has its
own goal; the purpose of the first is to get rid of false spirits, the second
to receive the true spirits, and the third to arise as a new person with
social and spiritual authority.

A. "Huten-Kut" (False Gods Ritual)
"Huten-spirits" is a general name for the stray, false, and evil
spirits. They are the spirits of *han* that are hovering over the world,
unable to leave for their journey to the other world. Their *han* must be
resolved, before they are ready for the journey. In the "huten-kut"
ritual, the initiating shaman begins with a period of dancing while
carrying a basket on her head containing white beans, millet, a piece of
hemp cloth, and a few pieces of three colored cloth. She then throws the

basket backward over her head, repeating this until it lands upright. If the basket lands facing down, it means the false or stray spirits are still hungry and still in need of receiving food. When the basket lands upright, it means that the false spirits are sated and thus able to embark on the journey to the other world.

In Korean Shamanism the items in the basket, which are offerings to the "huten-spirits," have their various symbolic meanings; the beans and millet represent food for the evil spirits, and the piece of hemp cloth represents the purification of the uncleanlines of death. The pieces of colored cloth contain the wish for the opening of the way to the other world.[60]

To resolve their *han*, they must be fed their favorite food, for hunger is considered an important contributor of *han*. The experience of hunger in the long history of the Korean people is reflected in this belief.[61] The psychological purpose of providing food for the evil spirit is to recognize the existence of unconscious complexes and pay serious attention to their neglected and repressed demands. Psychological insights are contained in this aspect of Korean Shamanism, in which even evil spirits are treated nicely through offerings of food and entertainment, so that they can leave peacefully. One insight is that evil is attracted to a person who could not live his life fully, for whatever reason. The way the shaman deals with the evil spirits is another wisdom of Korean Shamanism, with its belief that if attention and care are given to the neglected aspects of ourselves, they become less threatening and more helpful to us.

The piece of hemp cloth is thought of in Korean Shamanism as a purifying object whose function is to defend against the uncleanliness of death.[62] Through this symbol, *han* is equated with uncleanliness of the mind, the source of which is the fear of death. The "huten-spirits" are unclean and contaminated by the fear of death. Only when they are purified can they pass through the gate of the death without being harmed. This process of purification can be compared with the process of working through the contents of the unconscious complexes. This process includes the reactivating of forgotten and repressed wounds, that is, reexperiencing pain and suffering. This type of suffering is qualitatively different from the suffering exacted by *han* as the price for refusing to suffer legitimately. Authentic, conscious suffering has the saving power to liberate the individual from falsified suffering. The psychological meaning of this process is, as Bou-yong Rhie suggests, the establishment of a new relationship with one's unconscious through actively bringing to consciousness the contents of one's "shadow."[63]

The pieces of colored cloth symbolize the opening of the way and the solution to the predicament of stray spirits. Though they are nurtured and purified, they are still imprisoned in the old world, unable to separate themselves from old ties and influences. What they need is to break out of their prison, through the opening to the new world. The "gilgarem" (opening a way ritual) in "Chinogi-kut" (calming stray soul ritual) or "Dari-kut" (bridge ritual), with its decisive action of cutting the cotton cloth, is the symbolic expression of the break through imprisonment. Once the spirits leave this world and cross the bridge between this world and the other, they cannot come back. The symbolic action of cloth-cutting has two meanings that are paradoxical. One, the opening of the way to liberate the imprisoned souls to go freely into their own world. Two, the closing of the way to block the return of the souls to this world, nor to the persons with whom they have been identified.

Chi-ha Kim, a Korean poet and an original contributor to the formation of Minjung Theology in the 1970's, derives his philosophy of "dan" from the image of "cutting."[64] He finds the solution for the problem of *han* in the practice of "dan," in which one cuts oneself off from "every comfort and the easy life, circles of petite bourgeois dreams, and secular swamps without depth." He also believes that in the practice of "dan," the vicious circle of *han* can be broken.[65] In his philosophy of "dan" Chi-ha Kim, who considers himself a priest of *han* in the traditional role of a shaman, is in a sense performing the ritual of "cutting."

"Cutting" is an aggressive action required to break the old world which imprisons the victim. Under the influence of *han*, aggression is repressed and becomes an unavailable source of energy. When the unclean part of the unconscious is purified through the conscious effort of reexperiencing the sufferings of the past, aggression is at last available to energize one's courage and strength to break through one's fixation. As Jung suggests, only boldness can deliver from fear, and from the spirit of evil.[66]

Wilfried Daim, a Vienese psychoanalyst who is also an ardent Catholic, discusses the importance of breaking through the fixation at a certain stage of the treatment of a neurosis. According to him, the treatment of the neurosis has a phase of liberation from idolatrous fixation. The neurotic sufferer has the "object of fixation" which has absolute value for him. It acts within his personality like a god, but it is a false absolute, which must be abandoned.[67] This observation applies to the problem of the fixation of *han*. The sufferer of *han* tends to become idol worshiper fixated with a world view or ideology that is extremely narrow and constricting. He identifies increasingly with the object of fixation so that giving up the object becomes more and more difficult. That accounts for the need for aggression to break the idolatry, the narrowly constricting world view, and the "circles of petite bourgeois dream."[68] In this sense, aggression plays a redemptive role, destroying the idol's power and tearing apart its illusory world.

The symbolic action of "cutting," however, should not be misunderstood to be the single heroic action of cutting oneself off from the old world. As Ann and Barry Ulanov point out, "neurosis can occur if a person cuts himself off too sharply from his past, trying to overcome it rather than to outgrow it or build upon it."[69] One should not attempt to cut off the old world of "huten spirits" without first purifying them. Furthermore, they cannot be purified until they are nurtured and become healthy. The "cutting" should be understood as the outcome of the growth of the new personality and its new world view, than as the elimination of the old personality and world view, leaving a vacuum in its place. The process of "huten-kut" is a preparation for entering the next stage of the establishment of a new identity, without which the elimination of the false world view may result in a bigger misery.

B. "Naerim-Kut" (The Initiation Ritual)

There are six steps in the "naerim-kut." First, the prospective shaman pronounces the names of the gods that descend to her. She enters into a special relation with several gods from the traditional pool of gods by naming them. She then has to find the "bonsaek" (identity) of the gods. This is done by finding the right costume for each god who has become her personal god. Usually she receives more than one god.[70]

Second, the prospective shaman has to find the shaman bell and fan that were hidden at the beginning of the ritual. She continues to search while dancing until she finds the hidden treasures.

The third step is the "malmoon-yulgi" (opening the tongue), which is speaking the "kongsoo," the word of god. The "kongsoo" is a form of prophecy, including words of resentment, admonition, and blessings. The prospective shaman gives her first "kongsoo" to the participants in the ritual.

As the fourth step, the prospective shaman selects a few of the seven covered bowls containing either water, rice, ash, beans, forage, rice-washed water, or money. In the traditional understanding, each of these bowls has its own symbolic meaning: water represents lif; rice represents the blesssing for all people; ash represents purification of mind; the beans, forage and rice-washed water represent the prosperity of livestock; and money represents wealth. Her choices are interpreted as signs of her special gifts as a shaman. If she picks the bowl of ash, for example, she must be specially gifted at purifying minds.

The fifth step is to confirm that the prospective shaman is qualified as a shaman in every way. Her hair is remade after being loosened, while the administering shaman blesses her by sprinkling water on her head with the branch of a palm tree and singing. The content of her song is mainly blessing and admonition including phrases such as: "false spirits are all gone," "keep your mind clean," "take care of the people on earth," "bring prosperity to them," etc..[71]

The last step is to receive the shaman bell and the shaman fan from the administering shaman, who throws them to the initiate while singing.

The song contains lessons for the new shaman. She is admonished to keep her mind pure, to love even enemies, to endure hardships, and to continue the journey through the way of righteousness and goodness.[72]

The steps of "naerim-kut" represent the process of establishing a new identity of a shaman after resolving the *han* and the old false identity. By naming the gods and finding their costumes, the shaman prospect clarifies the relationship with the gods that possess her. Through this her personal gods are identified with the cultural gods, and her personal identity acquires a new meaning in relation to society and its culture. With this process her trance is endowed with order and a sense of purpose, and becomes a useful tool for the service of society.

The psychological explanation for the gods can be found in Jung's concept of archetypes. When the shadow part of the complexes are purified, one can enter the relationship with the archetypes, which are the sources of life. The archetypes always borrow their concrete forms of representation from cultural tradition. The cultural gods are the images of the archetypes grown in the specific soil of history and culture. The costumes of gods should not be changed as one changes attire, as that they are living symbols rooted in the unconscious of the people. Symbols always wear their cultural clothes, which are unique to their culture. On the importance of authentic cultural collective symbols Jung emphasizes as follows;

> Shall we be able to put on, like a new suit of clothes, ready-made symbols grown on foreign soil saturated with foreign blood, spoken in a foreign tongue, nourished by a foreign culture, interwoven with foreign history, and so resemble a beggar who wraps himself in kingly raiment, a king who disguises himself as a beggar? No doubt this is possible. Or is there something in ourselves that commands us to go in for no mummeries, but perhaps even to sew our garment ourselves? If we now try to cover our nakedness with the gorgeous trappings of the East, as the theosophists do, we would be playing our own history false.[73]

The psychic layer of the collective unconscious, which Jung discovers to be universal across cultures, exists in reality only in the realm of culture, because those images of the archetypes grow in the soil of a specific culture and its history. Any attempt at replacing the symbols of deities, which are indigenous to its own culture, with those that are grown in a foreign culture and history, may cause psychological and spiritual poverty to the life of the individuals of the society. For example, Korean Christianity, in replacing the original cultural symbols with those grown in the Judaeo-Christian tradition, is experiencing "a state of split" between the conscious and the unconscious. Korean Christians, who are still drawing emotional energy from Shamanism in their experiential level, are unable to use this energy on a conscious and ethical level. In their conscious mind they are Christians, having Christian terminologies and dogmas, while in their unconscious they still belong to Korean Shamanism.[74] Knowing the correct names and proper costumes of the cultural gods, therefore, is a significant task in building one's identity in his or her culture.

The bell and fan, the two most important emblems of the shaman, represent spiritual power. The bell with its sound is believed to have power to drive away evil spirits, and the fan has the power to create wind, which is a known symbol of spirits. Finding these emblems is related to finding professional identity in society as a shaman.[75]

The demonstration of the ability to prophecy is the most conspicuous sign that she can read and verbalize the contents of the unconscious. With this capacity she communicates with gods and spirits and create meaning and order in place of chaos and confusion.

The seven bowls represent the needs in everyday life for both human and animal. The third part of the rite shows that the function of the shaman is to take care of people in their real life situation with its daily suffering. The object of her care even extends to the welfare of livestock.

The climax of the "naerim-kut" is found in the re-doing of the shaman's hair. This symbolizes the "*hieros gamos*," the union with the god through marriage. It resembles the custom of the traditional marriage when the bridegroom loosens the bride's hair by taking off the "binyu" (a traditional hair pin) on the wedding night just before going into the bed. Bou-yong Rhie understands the essence of "naerim-kut" as the union with the "momjoo" (the shaman's personal god). He views the "momjoo" as the archetype of animus of the shaman.[76]

The song of the administering shaman makes clear the vocation of the novice, who is called to serve the gods and people with a pure and caring heart. For this purpose she receives the public vocation of shaman, which is symbolized by receiving the bell and fan.

C. "Sosle Kut" (Emergence Ritual)

The "sosle-kut" is the coda to the ritual of "naerim-kut." Here the new shaman publicly shows her newly acquired supernatural powers by dancing on the blade of "jagdoo" (a grass-cutting tool) placed about 10 feet above the ground. This is one way she proves the existence of the gods and their power. She is elevated to a professional religious leader and healer, as she actually rises high and dances on the blade. The purpose of this action is to prove the purified and sanctified body and mind of the shaman. Now she cannot be harmed or contaminated by evil. The blade of the cutter on which the shaman dances is related to the symbolic meaning of "gilgarem," in which the shaman's act of cutting has the central significance. By dancing on the edge of the cutting blade she demonstrates her capacity to cut and liberate the imprisoned souls.

In summary, despite the complexities of the rituals, the basic inner process of the initiation ritual is psychologically equivalent to that of the "Barikongjoo" myth. The first process is to resolve the shell part of the personal complex, which can also be called *han* in the narrower sense of the meaning. Next, to establish relationships with the archetypes. Finally to become a person of vocation. The resolution of *han* is one part of this whole process of the transformation of the personality. The meaning of *han*, therefore, should be found in its relation to the whole process of the transformation of the personality. *Han* is the starting point for the journey of psychological and spiritual growth. It is the gate to enter the realm of Being, because through *han* one encounters the archetypes, the symbolic representations of God. Through its symptoms, *han* forces people to open their eyes to the wounds in their psyches, and thus impels them start the journey of healing. The negative energy of *han* is now used as the source for creative energy in the cultural realm.

CHAPTER VI

THE *HAN* IN KOREAN MINJUNG THEOLOGY

1. Minjung Theology and *Han*

Minjung Theology is an indigenous Christian theology of the Korean people, emerged in the historical and cultural context of Korea in the 1970's. "Min" literally means "the people" and "jung" "the mass." Thus, the general meaning of the word *minjung* is the mass of people.[1] But the word *minjung,* cannot simply be rendered as the general definition of "mass of people," because of its emphasis on the consciousness of the oppressive social reality. Various definitions have been proposed for the term *minjung.* First, *minjung* are those who are oppressed politically, exploited economically, alienated socially, and kept uneducated in cultural and intellectual matters.[2] Second, *minjung* are those who have been treated as mere objects by those in power throughout history but, paradoxically, who have been the true subjects of history and the carriers of culture.[3] Third, *minjung* can be identified with those "Ochlos" whom Jesus favored, identified with and chose as the heirs to his kingdom in the Gospel of Mark.[4]

The understanding of the word *minjung* is incomplete until it is seen in relation to the meaning of *han*, because the inner reality of *minjung* is *han*. *Minjung* are those who have *han*. Social categorizations of "*minjung*," such as powerful vs. powerless, oppressor vs. oppressed, haves vs. have-nots, and learned vs. unlearned, cannot encompass the essence of *minjung*. When Byung-mu Ahn suggests the indefinability of the word *minjung* on the grounds that it is a holistic, dynamic and changing reality which escapes categorization, he seems to acknowledge the insufficiency of these socio-economic categorizations of *minjung*.

Minjung Theology was born out of the experience of *han*. A brief sketch of the beginning of Minjung Theology will make this evident. The Christian social activity in Korea in the early 1960's was centered on the issue of human rights for factory workers. Those Christian social activists struggled to combat abuses at the work place and to advance the workers' human rights. In the late 1960's the focus of the movement switched from the issue of human rights to the issue of social justice. It became the struggle to combat social injustice supported by the immoral military dictatorship. They began to see that the unjust social, political, and economic system was responsible for the misery of factory workers. Until these activists were exposed to the extreme suffering of the workers, there was no need for a new theology. The extent of this suffering, which was called *han*, was expressed in the factory workers' radical forms of protest, such as Tae-il Chun's self-immolation, which marks the turning point from the human rights movement to the Minjung movement.[5] The *han* of the factory workers challenged a group of theologians and opened their eyes to reality from a new perspective. Most Minjung theologians view the death of Tae-il Chun as the starting point of Minjung Theology.[6] Nam-dong Suh views that Minjung Theology started from reflection upon the experience of *han*. Accordingly, it can be claimed, that any discussion of Minjung Theology that has not evolved from reflection upon the experience of *han*, has nothing to do with Minjung Theology, no matter how similar it may look on the surface. This view is shared by Dong-hwan Moon who claims that *han* initiates a radical new starting point.

> *Han* . . . is a starting point for a new human history. Through
> the experience of *han* one's spiritual eyes are opened and one
> is enabled to see the deeper truth about life. In *han* we see
> clearly what is good and evil and learn to hate evil and love
> good. In *han* we encounter God who comes down to the
> *han*-ridden people and justifies their plight.[7]

With the discovery of *han*, Minjung theologians started a new
indigenous Korean theology. They realized the traditional theology
evolved in the West was inappropriate to address the reality of *han*,
grown in Korean soil. This realization led to a liberation from western
theology, which in turn enabled them to start a new theology. Their
excitement over this liberation and the discovery of a new treasure is
vividly depicted in Nam-dong Suh's remarks in his article "Towards the
Theology of *Han*";

> Let me conclude by making an appeal to my fellow
> theologians in Korea. Let us hold in abeyance discussion on
> doctrines and theories about sin which are heavily charged
> with the bias of ruling class and are often nothing more than
> the labels the ruling class uses for the deprived. Instead, we
> should take *han* as our theme, which is indeed the language of
> the *minjung* and signifies the reality of their experience. If one
> does not hear the sighs of the *han* of the *minjung*, one cannot
> hear the voice of Christ knocking on our door.[8]

Through *han*, Minjung Theology could meet the tradition of Korean
culture and history in a different way. A genuine encounter between
Christian theology and the Korean cultural and historical tradition had
not been made until the arrival of Minjung Theology, which discovered
the *han* as its central theme. Korean Indigenization Theology, which had
been tried to deal with the Korean cultural tradition seriously, could not
overcome the barriers of religious dogma. Postulating the basic analogy
between Christianity and the Korean culture as "seed" to "soil," its goal
was to plant the seed of life, the Gospel of the Christian church, in the

soil of the Korean culture and mind. With this analogy, the supremacy of Christianity over the Korean cultural tradition was maintained. The image of "seedless soil" betrayed the belief that Korean history and culture did not belong to the realm of God's love, or at best had only a secondary importance compared to that of the Judaeo-Christian tradition, and this turned out to be a barrier in the relationship between the Indigenization Theology and Korean culture. Through the experience of liberation from the western theology, Minjung theologians could overcome this barrier and encounter their cultural tradition on a different horizon. They could discover and witness God's presence in the history of the Korean people and their experience of life. For example, Yong-hak Hyun's theological explication of the Korean mask dance opened a new realm in which Korean culture and Christian theology could genuinely acquaint. Hyun claims, long before the introduction of Christianity, Korean *minjung* could encounter God in their experiences of "critical transcendence" during the traditional mask dance.[9]

This does not mean that they chose the Korean tradition as an alternative to traditional Christianity. On the contrary, by becoming liberated from the western theology, they could understand more clearly the meaning of the history of God, as revealed in the Old and the New Testaments and in the world church history. They realized their newly found God was indeed the God of all human beings and not just the God of Israel or of Korea.

2. The Interpretations of *Han* in Minjung Theology

(1) *Han* as Feelings

Minjung theologians understand *han* as feelings more than anything else. For them, *han* is an underlying feeling of the Korean people. It is a feeling of defeat, resignation, and nothingness (Nam-dong Suh), grudge or resentment (Dong-hwan Moon), angry and sad sentiments turned inward (Chi-ha Kim), helplessness and hopelessness (Kwang-sun Suh). These perceptions of the *han* feeling are based on the understanding of *han* in the Korean cultural tradition. Anger, grudge, and resentment are the main attributes of the "wonhan" feeling, whereas defeat, resignation, emptiness, helplessness, hopelessness, loneliness, longing for the loved one, and sadness are the attributes of "jeong-han."

(2) *Han*, the Suppressed and Repressed Feelings

In Minjung Theology, *han* is understood as both a suppressed and repressed feeling. Most Minjung theologians understand *han* as feelings caused by the subject's suppression of his feelings in the face of external oppression. Chi-ha Kim views that *han* is "caused when one's outgoingness is blocked and suppressed for an extended period of time by external oppression and exploitation."[10] Kwang-sun Suh includes the aspect of repression as well as suppression. He relates repression to the *han* of the individual and suppression (or oppression) to collective *han* on a social and political level. According to him, "the feeling of *han* is not just an individual feeling of repression . . . This is a collective feeling of the oppressed . . . The feeling of *han* is an awareness both at an individual psychological level as well as at a social and political level."[11] Despite the inclusion of the repressed feeling caused by the psychological condition, emphasis is given to the suppressed feeling caused by the social and political condition. External condition is believed to form the contents of the collective *han*, which is the central concern of Minjung Theology.

(3) *Han*, the Subjective vs. Objective Experience

In Minjung Theology, *han* is not only understood as feeling but also as an experience. *Han* is an accumulation of the suppressed and condensed experience of oppression.[12] This understanding of *han* as a cluster of experiences of suffering, which is more than just a suppressed or repressed feeling, reveals that Minjung theologians are aware of the psychic reality of *han*, which forms the structural basis of the *han* feeling in the personality. When Nam-dong Suh explains that "*han* is the suppressed, amassed and condensed experience of oppression, caused by mischief or misfortune, so that it forms kind of 'lump' in one's spirit,"[13] he is aware of the existence of a psychic reality similar to the concept of the "original wounds" in one's personality.

Thus, Minjung theologians acknowledge that the concrete basis of the living *han* does exist in individuals.[14] They discuss the *han* of individuals. But they concern more on the societal aspects of *han* in their dealing with the *han* of individuals. Nam-dong Suh finds in the death of Kyung-sook Kim the collective *han* of the Korean workers. He reports about Kyung-sook Kim's suffering as follows.

> Miss Kim was an executive committee member of the Y.H. Trade Union and was a leader in initiation the demonstrations and rallies, composing and reading statements and appeals. According to the letter she left for her mother and younger brother, in her eight years of experience as a factory worker, she had had innumerable nosebleeds from exhaustion, and she sometimes worked three months without being paid. She had to live on, struggling with near-starvation, inadequate clothing, no heat in winter, and often she had only small 30-won cakes to eat for a meal . . . Finally, at 2 a.m. on August 11, during a forced dispersal of the workers by a 1,000 strong police force, Miss Kim Kyung-Sook (21 years old) was killed.[15]

Nam-dong Suh claims that, in the death of Miss Kim were concentrated the various contradictions of political and economic structures, and her death embodies the *han* of eight million Korean workers.[16] In this interpretation, the *han* of Miss Kim contains both the socio-political and personal aspects of *han*, with its emphasis on the socio-political side. Though *han* has socio-political aspect, *han* is the subjective experience of the *minjung,* who is not an object, the product of social condition, but a subject, who can creatively respond to any given conditions. Any experience of *han* should therefore be interpreted as a personal and subjective experience before being interpreted as an index of social conditions. The insight of Minjung Theology, that *minjung* are not the objects of history but the subjects of it, should be applied to the interpretation of the *han* of individuals.[17] *Minjung*'s experience of *han* is a subjective experience. They have maintained their dignity and creativity, both in health and in pathology, even under circumstances of extreme oppression. *Han* is the very product of one's subjectivity created in the attempt to cope with the external and internal, real and phantasmal, oppressors in one's life. The collective *han* should be understood not as a direct result of external circumstances but as the product of the subjectivity of the people through their personal experience of external challenges. A tendency to identify the objective, social condition with the subjective *han* is seen when Nam-dong Suh suggests the "fourfold *han*" of the Korean people.

> 1. Koreans have suffered numerous invasions by surrounding powerful nations so that the very existence of the Korean nation has come to be understood as *han*.
> 2. Koreans have continually suffered the tyranny of the rulers so that they think of their existence as "backsung."[18]
> 3. Also, under Confucianism's strict imposition of laws and customs discriminating against women, the existence of women was *han* itself.
> 4. At a certain point in Korean history, about half of the population was registered as hereditary slaves, and were treated as property rather than as people of the nation. These thought of their lives as *han*. These four may be called the Fourfold *han* of the Korean people.[19]

If *han* is objectified by being identified with historical and social conditions, *minjung* becomes the object of history than the subject of it. Thus the fourfold *han* suggested by Nam-dong Suh should be understood as the fourfold social conditions of *han* of the Korean people.

(4) The Negative vs. Positive Aspects of *Han*

The negative aspect of *han* is acknowledged by most Minjung theologians, especially by Kwang-sun Suh and Chi-ha Kim. Suh describes, "The feeling of *han* . . . also has a negative element. It is a repressed murmuring, unexpressed in words or actions. It does not change anything. It might arouse a sense of revenge at most."[20] He also acknowledges the insights of the psychoanalysts who view *han* as the psychological basis of schizophrenia and other psychosomatic illnesses of the Korean people.[21] It is Chi-ha Kim who seems most keenly aware of the negative aspect of *han* when he describes *han* as something "fearful which can kill, destroy, and hate endlessly . . . *Han*, separating itself from human emotion, becomes substantial and grows into a ghostly creature. It appears as a concrete substance with enormous ugly and evil energy."[22]

The main concern of Minjung Theology is not the exploration of the negative aspect of *han*, but of the positive aspect of it. Nam-dong Suh's interpretation exemplifies this.

> On the one hand, it is a dominant feeling of defeat, resignation and nothingness. On the other, it is a feeling with a tenacity of will for life which comes to weaker beings. The first aspect can sometimes be sublimated to great artistic expressions and the second aspect could erupt as the energy for a revolution or rebellion.[23]

Both aspects are positive, because they can be sublimated to the expression of art or to the energy to change social reality. The insights of Dong-hwan moon shed even further light on the positive aspect of *han*. For him, *han* is a starting point of a new human history. It brings us to an understanding of the deeper truth of life, teaches us to love good and hate evil, and finally brings us to an encounter with God.[24] The positive aspect of *han* is most beautifully expressed in Young-hak Hyun's exposition of the transcendent experience of *han* during the mask dance. According to him, a sublimation of *han* takes place in the experience of "critical transcendence" that comes to people at the climax of the mask dance. This experience produces two positive effects:

> First, it creates among the *minjung* the wisdom and the power to survive . . . They are able to bear the hardships of the world with good humor. This is especially true in times when there seems to be no exit, no possibility for effective change. Second, the experience provides the *minjung* with the courage to fight for change and freedom . . . And that happens without much self-righteousness, for this experience of critical transcendence places them not only over against

others who oppress the *minjung* but also over against the *minjung* themselves.[25]

The enlightenment of the positive aspects of *han* by Minjung theologians is considered to be an invaluable contribution to the understanding of *han*. Nonetheless, it must be pointed out that by avoiding an examination of the negative aspect of *han* and by concentrating only on its positive aspect, Minjung theologians are liable to lose the balance in their understanding of *han*. This lack of balance may in turn cause a lack of discernment among the different entities of *han*. The experience of *han* that Chi-ha Kim addresses is that of "wonhan," whereas the *han* in the mask dance that Young-hak Hyun explores belongs to the category of "jeong-han."

Minjung theologians find in the death of Tae-il Chun the most sacred aspect of *han* because, they believe, it is death of self-sacrifice. Nam-dong Suh depicts the death of Chun as a replica of the sacrificial death of Jesus that is reincarnated in Korean history. A record of Chun's diary written three months before he committed suicide, during the labor movement protest shows his wish to sacrifice himself for those he loved.

> At this moment I have made an almost absolute decision. I must return. I must return without failure. To the home of my heart where my poor brothers and sisters are . . . To the young hearts of the Peace Market which is my ideal place. I have sworn to my life in the long hours of fantasy to go to you who are weak beings and in need of care. I will desert myself and kill myself to go to you. Endure a little longer. I will sacrifice my weak self to stay with you. You are the home of my soul . . . Today is Saturday. The second Saturday of August. The day I made up my mind. Dear God, have compassion and mercy on me as I strive to become a drop of dew.[26]

Nam-dong Suh interprets Chun's death as a noble death. He claims that "The life of Tae-il Chun was to liberate the life of the weaker beings from their pains and exploitations, by absorbing their pains and unjust exploitations in himself. The answer to the question about the true life is revealed in this sacrifice."[27] This interpretation, however, raises a serious question; Can we ethically and theologically justify or praise the act of killing oneself in the name of justice, *minjung*, or even God?

Seen from the depth psychological point of view, self-immolation, whether of student or factory worker, can be considered the clearest example of the manifestation of the negative aspect of *han*. The *han* of Tae-il Chun had a deeper root in himself than just in the unjust exploitive working conditions in Peace Market. He had his own world of fantasy in which he decided to kill himself to return to where his loving brothers and sisters were waiting for him. It is a tragedy that he burnt himself and this tragic aspect should not be denied nor idealized. As is already shown in the analyses of the *han* of Eun Ko and So-wol Kim, the impulse to commit suicide arises in the *han*-ridden psyche as a negative element of the nature of *han*. The same impulse can be discerned in Chun's fantasy, in which he decides to kill himself to return to his inner ideal love object which, in his case, is identified with the factory workers in Peace Market. If Chun's self-immolation is the realization of his fantasy in the socioeconomic scene, as is implied in his diary, then our urgent task should be for the prevention of further such occurrence, rather than reinforcing the fervent suicidal wish by idealizing it as religious, redemptive death.

In dealing with the symbols arising from the root of *han*, Minjung Theology seems lack the distinction between the healthy symbols that deserve to be lifted up to the level of social or religious symbol, and the unhealthy symbols originated from individual or collective pathologies. Often creativity expresses itself through pathology. It is important to recognize the creativity mixed with pathological phenomena. It is also important to recognize the pathology hidden in creative works. To use a creative but pathological symbol in the social realm is potentially dangerous to the psychic environment of society, let alone to the healing process of the particular individual involved.

(5) A Political Interpretation of *Han*

Because Minjung theologians experienced political oppression in their struggle against it, they are sensitive to the political aspect of social reality. According to Kwang-sun Suh's definition, Minjung Theology is "a political hermeneutics of the Gospel and a political interpretation of the Korean Christian experiences."[28] According to Nam-dong Suh, the most important element in the political consciousness of the *minjung* is *han*. *Han* is interpreted as "a deep awareness of the contradictions in a situation and of the unjust treatment meted out to the people or a person by the powerful."[29] This interpretation, however, is contradictory to the traditional understanding of *han*. In which, *han* is believed to be the very element that makes it impossible for individuals to have a conscious awareness of the contradictions in a situation, by making them prisoners of their own negative emotions and ideas based on fantasies than on realistic perception of the social reality. It seems that the *han* in which Minjung Theology discovers the seed of political consciousness is qualitatively different from the *han* generally conceived of among the Korean people. The *han* of Minjung Theology presupposes *minjung*'s capacity to discern multiple aspects of social reality and to make an ethical judgement, based on conscious awareness than on compulsive emotions. This *han* requires in *minjung* a psychic structure that is integrated as a whole. It can be identified as a mature "jeong-han."

Although "jeong-han" in its premature form can be a source of pathology individually and collectively, in its mature form it can also be the source of individual creativity as well as of social development. In contrast, "wonhan" or "huhan" which are rooted in a psychic structure that is marked with the primitive ego mechanisms of splitting, excessive projection, suicidal wish, etc., can only bring in a political consciousness that is conditioned by the nature of its fantasy. Therefore, the transformation from "wonhan" to mature "jeong-han" is the precondition for the political consciousness, which is capable of discerning the multiple aspects of social reality and of making ethical judgements based upon that discernment.

An insight Minjung Theology brought into the realm of political reality is that the core of social justice lay in the *han* of *minjung*. Justice does not come from intellectual ideas alone, but from the depths of the *minjung*'s heart. The cry for justice may be heard in the thoughts of scholars, but not as powerfully as in the stories of the *han* of *minjung*. A logical extension of this insight is that social justice depends upon the quality of the *han* of *minjung*. If their *han* is healed and transformed, it can become the very source of power to transform the society. This crucial insight, however, is overshadowed by the urgent concern of Minjung Theology. It is to use the energy of *han* for political revolution. The cry of *han* for justice, is interpreted as a cry for political action that can bring the resolution of *han*. According to Nam-dong Suh, *han* is "a tendency for social revolution,"[30] as expressed in the occurrences of rebellion and revolution in Korean history. This tendency toward revolution is cherished by Minjung theologians as the most important element of *han*; thus *han* is interpreted as the expression of *minjung*'s yearning for justice.

But here arises a question. Are all rebellions and revolutions expressions of the yearning for justice? It seems that, if the wounds of *han* are deep and unhealed, the tendency of *han* toward revolution is more likely a yearning for justice, that could bring with it, more injustice and thus more negative *han*. The tendency toward revolution that has its core in the yearning for justice applies only to the phenomenon of mature "jeong-han," whereas the tendency toward revolution that originates from the yearning for revenge is an expression of "wonhan" or "huhan." Although in actual revolution both unconscious tendencies coexist and create and inner tension, it is possible to discern whether the main tendency is one of justice or revenge.

Through a political interpretation of *han*, Minjung Theology focuses on the political aspect of reality that contributed to the formation of *han* in *minjung*. It sometimes goes beyond interpretation to the recreation of the story of *han* from its own perspective. For instance, the "Emille Bell" legend is recreated in Minjung Theology;

> During the Silla Kingdom, the devout Buddhist Queen, Sunduk (Good Virtue), wanted to make a huge bell as a sign of the poeple's dedication to Buddha. In return, Buddha would then protect the nation from foreign invasions. The bell was to be placed in the nation Buddhist temple in Kyungju. The Best bell maker was appointed by the Queen to

build the best bell in the world. He did everything right but
failed to make the bell produce the finest sound. He then
consulted the religious leaders appointed by the Queen. They
felt that a pure young maiden should be melted into the bell
in order to produce the finest sound. By the order of the
Queen, soldiers went out to fetch a pure young maiden. On
a poor farm village deep in the mountains they found a
mother who held a child. The soldiers took away the child,
who was crying, "Emille, Emille (Mother, Mother)." The
child was thrown into the melted iron that became the bell.
Afterward the bell produced the sweetest and finest sound.
The name of this bell came to be known as the bell of
Emille, because the beautiful sound ends with "Emille,
Emille, Emille (Mother, Mother, Mother)." It is the sound of
the child who calls her mother. The mother who hears it
cries. The sound of Emille Bell then, is the voice of *han*, the
han of Korean women and children, that is, the *han* of
minjung.[31]

The "Emille Bell" story re-created by Minjung Theology can be
compared with the more generally accepted version of the story;

To cast a huge bell many Buddhist monks had to make a tour
of the country to raise funds. One of the monks who traveled
throughout the country house to house knocked at the gate of
a destitute farmer. To the visiting monk, the matron of the
house said that, being so poor, she had nothing to contribute
but an infant daughter. The monk wrote down what the
woman offered in his donation book. Later when the casting
of the bell was begun it was decided that a human sacrifice
was necessary. So the infant daughter of the destitute farm
woman was brought and thrown into the pot of melted
copper. The bell was finally cast and responded to being
struck with a mournful tolling which reminded one of a baby
crying "emille... emille..." Hence the name of the bell became
"Emille" (meaning Mommy).[32]

In the original story, the baby is promised as sacrifice voluntarily, though carelessly, by its mother. Whereas in the new version of the story the baby is simply taken away by the soldiers to be sacrificed under the Queen's order. Nam-dong Suh views that these traditional interpretations have not succeeded in revealing the political aspect of the story. Behind the cunning monk who took advantage of the naive mother and her innocent words, a cruel political power was hidden. With a political interpretation, this hidden aspect can be clearly revealed. In Minjung Theology the *han* of "Emille Bell" is interpreted as the *han* of the powerless *minjung* protesting against the political power symbolized by the Queen and her soldiers.

The *han* of the "Emille Bell," however, is not exhausted by a political interpretation because its sound is primarily heard as the cry of the baby directed toward its mother. The poignancy of the *han* of "Emille Bell" lies in this aspect of immediacy between mother and baby. Yul-kyu Kim claims that the story of "Emille Bell" can be considered as a protest against the tragic infant-sacrifice.[33] The bell sound, Emille, should be heard as the voice of thousands of babies sacrificed under the name of religious devotion or of national security. The cry of the sacrificed baby can be heard as a protest against all kinds of social, political, and religious human sacrifice. The *han* of the baby cannot be sufficiently addressed in the framework of political interpretation. This apolitical aspect should be preserved even in a political interpretation of *han*. Otherwise the whole meaning of the story may be distorted.

The symbols contained in the legend should not be changed by anyone for practical needs. They are to grow and bloom in the minds of the people. By revising the story of the legend to make it better fit into the interpretive framework, the political interpretation of Minjung Theology can, in fact, discover in the *han* material only what it has projected onto it. Therefore, the political interpretation of *han* should be used in an inclusive, than an exclusive, reductionistic way to illuminate the political aspect of *han* without damaging its wholeness.

(6) The Internal vs. External Origin of *Han*

Most Minjung theologians believe that the origin of *han* lies in the external conditions of social contradiction and injustice, and the elimination of the external causes of *han* is the only possible way of resolving *han*. Based on this belief Nam-dong Suh criticizes the Korean shamanistic tradition, because while it resolves the *han* of people through shaman rituals, it never utilizes the *han* as the energy for social revolution, which is the only sure way to eliminate social problems.[34] For him, the positive element that might emerge out of the accumulation of the collective *han* of the oppressed people is in the transformation of *han* into a revolutionary activity.[35] Kwang-sun Suh agrees with this view, and says that the "sickness of *han* can be cured only when the total structure of the oppressed society is changed."[36] He believes that the original cause of *han* exists in the unjust social structure. Unless the evil in the social structure is eliminated, the *han* cannot be successfully resolved, because the *han*-creating condition remains unchanged. Minjung theologians believe, therefore, that the ultimate positive value of *han* is to be found in its transformation into energy for revolution. *Han* is to be utilized for revolution, than simply resolved, because social revolution is the true way of resolving *han*. In this view, the psychic reality of *han* becomes secondary while the reality of social evil, which exists in the socio-political arena, becomes of primary importance.

As a logical conclusion, Minjung theologians arrive at a belief that there is no evil in *han*. *Han* is an innocent victim. The people of *han* are innocent and sinless because they are only victims of the power of the evil that exists in the social structure. Byung-mu Ahn believes that *minjung* are the victims of a "sin complex" that was imposed on them by the oppressors, and thus their salvation comes not by liberation from sin but by liberation from the "sin complex". This can be achieved through the conscious realization of the evil structure of the society and a commitment to the cause of social revolution.

> The way of saving them (*minjung*) is not by the liberation from their sin but by the liberation from their "sin complex." This is the line of life that they primarily need. Also if they realize clearly the structure of the world which made them believe themselves sinners, and convert themselves to committed revolutionaries, they can leave the queue of sinners

to join the queue of *minjung* who are the subjects of world rescue.[37]

Seen from the psychological point of view, this line of reasoning is a shallow, if not false, understanding of *han*, in that *han* is believed to be something accumulated in the psyche that came only from the outside. That there is nothing inside the human mind that contributes to the creation of its psychic contents. The more assiduously people accept this view, and the more stubbornly they believe that all psychic contents have to come from the outside, the greater becomes their inner poverty. *Han* is more than the social contradictions and injustices that are introjected into the human mind. Further, the human mind is not a hollow container in which materials from the outside are accumulated, which can be eliminated from the mind just as a trash container is emptied. As Jung points out, "The psyche is the world's pivot: not only is it the one great condition for the existence of a world at all, it is also an intervention in the existing natural order, and no one can say with certainty where this intervention will finally end."[38] Whatever we experience in life is a psychic experience and is the creation of the psyche through a complex process of interaction with external reality. The feelings, images, and thoughts that constitute the inner material of the psychic experience are not something stuffed in from outside.

The idea that the complex is the product of only external oppression and is removable by devoting oneself to the cause of social justice, does not account for the inner nature of the complex. For Freud, complexes have their source in two basic instincts, the life instinct and the death instinct. Both of which are rooted in one's own psychological and biological endowment. Jung's theory of the complex shows that both positive and negative elements arise from the depths of one's own psyche in the process of the formation of the complex, and they are interwoven with a multitude of internal and external elements. Jung finds the psychic function, which he calls "shadow," arising from the deepest area of the psyche, the "collective unconscious." Although the materials of the shadow are interwoven with personal and historical experiences by one's interaction with external reality, the shadow is not just the result of personal experience in relation to external reality, but is a part of the archaic, primordial psychic materials out of which the human experiences of feelings, images, and thoughts are created.

On a deeper level, *han* is more than an ordinary complex. It is the original complex, the complex that is rooted in the basic structure of the personality. As is shown in the two position theory of Klein, *han* is in the basis of the personality and determines the future course of personality development. If we have the courage to look into the inner nature of *han* by looking into the depths of our own psyche instead of projecting the political reality of society onto the screen of *han* (or vice versa), we will be able to discern the root of evil in ourselves and especially in our *han*, in which our sin is revealed in its clearest form.

Han is not innocent. Innocent suffering is one cause of *han*, but once it becomes *han* it loses its innocence by becoming a source of evil forces that seek revenge on other innocent victims. *Han*, however, can be transformed, just as one's personality can be transformed, into a more mature form. Although there is a destructive instinct rooted in our own being, so that we are constantly reminded of our human nature, our personality can grow healthier and stronger in order to contain and transform that negative force into creative energy for art or for a better social reality. *Han*, therefore, is not simply to be eliminated nor used directly as the energy for social revolution, but is to be accepted and transformed into a different kind of psychic reality, possible only through the process of psychological and spiritual transformation.

Among Minjung theologians Dong-hwan Moon does try to find a deeper root of evil in the individual than in social injustice. Referring to the teachings of "Tonghak Religion" and Chi-ha Kim, Moon finds the root of evil in human greed. The "limitless appetite" and "greed" of the oppressor are responsible for the evil of the social structure and *han*. He also considers not only the rulers but also the hearts of the *minjung* similarly contaminated by greed, the very source of their *han*.[39] The root of evil is in the human greed of both the oppressor and the oppressed. He goes on to claim, however, that the source of evil is primarily in the greed of the oppressor than in that of oppressed. The greed of the oppressed is the secondary product which stems from being contaminated by the greed of the oppressor. Furthermore, the greed of the poor is different from that of the rich. In that the oppressed can save themselves from their greed, though it is not an easy task. This is because they have *han*, which can be a source of courage and power, to fight greed and evil. Oppressed people have the innate capacity to cleanse themselves of contamination, whereas the oppressor cannot help themselves, because they do not have the inner resources.[40] The root of all evil is not in the *han* of the oppressed but in the greed of oppressor. Therefore, despite the fact that *han* may be contaminated by greed, it does not become the source of evil. *Han*, essentially, has no evil in it.

This view hardly addresses the psychological reality of *han*. Seen from a psychological perspective greed, the root of evil, exists in *han*. Especially in "wonhan" and "huhan," regardless of social status. As Melanie Klein shows, greed is a derivative of destructive force that stems from human nature itself.[41] In Korean folktales, han is depicted as not only the victim of evil but also the creator of evil. The scheme of oppressor and oppressed does not fit with the psychological reality of *han*. The nature of the human psyche shows much more complex and dynamic reality than the simple dichotomy of oppressor and oppressed. If we consider the reality of *han* as something that has its own inner dynamics, and look into its negative and positive aspects to do justice to the reality of *han*, we will be able to discern the root of evil hidden in the *han* of both oppressor and oppressed. Greed, a major component of *han*, can be found not only in the desire of the oppressor but also in that of the oppressed. Thus the quest for the root of evil should consider both the factors of external and internal reality.

(7) *Han* and "Dan"

Most Minjung theologians accept Chi-ha Kim's idea of "dan" as an invaluable part of Minjung Theology, for it provides a way of overcoming the problem of *han*. According to Kim, *han* is responsible for the creation of a vicious circle of violence and repression, and this circle should be broken by the practice of "dan." The literal meaning of "dan" is "cutting off." On the personal level, "dan" is the practice of "self-denial" through which one can remove the temptation of the "easy life, circles of petite bourgeois dreams, and secular swamps without depth."[42] This idea is most clearly shown in Kim's prayer, written while he was in prison:

> Oh, God. I have been offering the same prayer for months.
> Listen to my prayer, Oh, Lord. Sharpen the sword in me.
> Grant me the courage to take the act of dan, if my heart
> bursts in pain, so that I can start the journey for the battlefield
> . . . Ah. Help me to cut off for the far away journey. I
> cannot cut off the tie that draws me into the flowery tomb of
> happy pleasurable home, the nest of amnesia. Help me to cut
> the little leafy hands and the blinking eyes of the meek
> woman. Help me cut, cut, cut off that tie. Send me off to the
> wilderness, dawning under the cold wintry stars, where I can
> obtain the maddeningly bitter awakenings.[43]

This prayer shows how desperately Kim is struggling with the inner forces that are pulling him down into a depressive mood, in which the happy home becomes a flowery tomb and the nest of amnesia. This inner force of *han*, he believes, can be cut off through the practice of "dan," which is a heroic act. With "dan" he is taking an active role against all the passivity, which means death to him. His goal is to move toward the "battlefield" and the "wilderness" where he can obtain "maddeningly bitter awakenings." What does this "battlefield" or "wilderness" mean? To him, it means revolution. Revolution is the ultimate resolution of his *han* and the *han* of *minjung*. By revolution he does not mean just a social and political revolution, but a total revolution in which a transformation from the present, lower spiritual state into a higher spiritual state takes place. To reach this higher spiritual state, both the energy of *han* and the will power of "dan" are needed. Without "dan," *han* will explode into a vicious circle of destruction. Chi-ha Kim is keenly aware of the negative forces of *han*, the impulsive wishes to hate, kill, destroy, and take revenge. If these forces of *han* are not harnessed by "dan," they will cause endless destruction. Only the *han* that is restrained by "dan" can bring about a total social, political, and spiritual revolution. Since negative forces constantly arise from *han*, a repetition of "dan" is necessary "to suppress the explosion that can break out of the vicious circle, so that *han* can be sublimated as higher spiritual power."[44]

"Dan" is to overcome *han*. In a collective sense, it means "to cut the vicious circle of revenge." For Kim, this does not mean to give up revolution. On the contrary, the practice of collective "dan" can be done only through revolution that, of course, includes socio-political revolution. Kim never underestimates the importance of socio-political revolution. His goal is to achieve both political and spiritual revolution at the same time. He declares:

> People's *han* and rage ought to be liberated from their
> masochistic exercise, to be a great and fervent clamor
> demanding for God's justice. If needed, it ought to be
> developed into a decisive and organized explosion. This
> miraculous transition lies in religious commitment and in
> internal and spiritual transformation.[45]

Kim does not explain how this kind of revolution takes place. It is "a miraculous transition" that resists any logical explanation. Several functions of "dan" are involved in this process of the transforming *han* into spiritual power for revolution. First, "dan" liberates *han* from its masochistic exercise and channels its energy into social revolution. Second, "dan" purifies the revengeful impulse to become a desire for God's justice. Third, "dan" organizes and controls the direction and the limits of the explosion of *han* in the revolution so that establishment of a new social reality based on justice becomes possible.

Limited violence is not only acceptable in this process but it is a necessary element to make this process possible. Kim says;

> The church ought to be the comforter to resolve the *han* of the
> *minjung* and to cut the vicious circle of violence, and to
> change it into a progressive movement. For this purpose,
> churches ought to accept limited violence, and ought to be a

sanctuary for radicals and fighters who are progressing out of
the dark.[46]

By "limited violence" he means an explosion of *han* limited by
"dan." He calls this type of violence "the violence of love." This
violence is not the violence of oppression, but of resistance. Not the
violence of depriving humanity, but of restoring it. He believes that in
essence this violence is identical with "the courageous non-violence."[47]

Without romanticizing the negative aspect of *han*, Kim firmly
believes in the possibility of the transformation of the quality of *han*
from "hate-aggression" to "love-aggression," from an impulse toward
revenge to a power for justice. His belief about the transformation of
han is also rooted in his love for the *minjung*, which is again rooted in
his religious commitment to God.[48] This belief can be supported by the
discoveries of depth psychology concerning the transformation from the
"paranoid-schizoid position" to the "depressive position," or from
"wonhan" and "huhan" to "jeong-han." Depth psychology can provide
details of the inner process of the transformation of *han*. The difference,
however, lies in their different ways of approaching the reality of *han*.
The approach of "dan" to the reality of *han* is through "cutting off" and
"self-denial," whereas the approach of depth psychology is through
"connection to" and "self-acceptance." In the practice of "dan" the
chains of associated images and their accompanying wishes, fantasies,
and feelings are cut off in the fashion of self-sacrifice. In the practice of
depth psychology the fragmented images, ideas, wishes, and feelings are
connected together in the search for self-restoration.

Despite their apparent differences, they do share certain common
elements. Both practices aim to look at the inner contents of *han*
knowingly, courageously, and honestly. Both practices try to sharpen
our attention to all of the parts of our psychic body, all the regions of
personality, and every part of the corporate body of our society. For
both practices the sharpening of awareness is crucial for the conscious
realization of the contents of *han*, before making any decision whether

to cut or to connect. When Kim prays to God, "sharpen the sword in me," he is praying for this same goal of sharpening one's awareness.

Seen from the depth psychological point of view, however, it has to be pointed out that Kim's approach entails a danger to the well-being of one's psyche and to others' well-being. It is true that Kim's practice of "dan" is a heroic one which only a few exceptionally strong minds can achieve. In his "dan," every root of the negative elements should be exposed and eradicated by the sharpened sword of consciousness. This sword is to kill the "beast" in one's self. Killing the "beast" is the act of "dan."[49] The wisdom from depth psychology suggests that the conscious ego, which is the agent of decision making, has its own limitations. One's ego can be scorched by the numinous power of the psyche if it is too closely touched by the "maddeningly bitter awakenings," which Kim seeks out. The ego has to learn to make peace with the other elements in the psyche, rather than to cut them off radically. The wisdom contained in the practice of Korean Shamanism would also suggest the same idea. It is wiser to reconcile the psychic forces arising from the depths of instinct, by treating them with care, than to fight them. In the oldest shaman story, when "Chu-yong," a legendary ancestor of a shaman, was confronted with evil, he dealt with it with humor and grace, through singing and dancing, instead of trying to kill it. Then he could overcome the evil that otherwise would have overpowered him.

> Late in the night I came home. I see four legs in my bed
> instead of two. Two are mine. Whose legs are the other two.
> What can I do when I see my wife is robbed.[50]

This suggestion does not deny the importance of struggle, decision making, and fighting that are important elements in the practice of "dan," but it does mean that there is a need for limiting their importance. In Korean folktales, help often comes from the instinctual side, symbolized by an animal such as a frog, cow, bird, etc..[51] In the myth of "Barikongjoo," only when Bari's inflated ego becomes humble can she accept and utilize the wisdom and power that comes from instinct.[52] Jung clearly indicates that "without the cooperation of the unconscious and its instinctive forces the conscious personality would be too weak to wrench itself from its infantile past and venture into a strange world with all its unforeseen possibilities. The whole of the libido is needed for the battle of life."[53] In Kim's prayer, the images of "sword," "battle field," "wilderness," and "cold wintry stars," that represent the masculine principle are depicted as desirable. The values that Kim is searching for are masculine values. His God is the masculine God who awaits him with a sharp sword, in a battlefield of wilderness under the cold wintry stars, to give him maddeningly bitter awakenings. His God is the God of justice and of revolution. The images of "happy home," "nest," and "the little hands and the eyes of woman" that represent the feminine principle, are depicted as the forces of temptation, corruption, and death that should be cut off. The happy home is like a tomb or a nest of amnesia, and the little leafy hands and the blinking eyes of the meek woman are things to be "cut, cut, and cut off."

When Kim talks about love in his philosophy of the "violence of love," it is a masculine love which accompanies violence. The meaning of the word "love" that he uses must be different from the ordinary meaning of love that is generally associated with the attributes of warmth, kindness, softness, forgiveness, and sweetness. He means, instead, coldness, cruelty, sharpness, justice, and bitterness. This masculine love may be a strong criticism of the sentimental and corrupted love that does not know the difference between justice and injustice. Kim's idea of "the violence of love" was his response to what he viewed as the corrupted feminine love that many Korean churches in those days were practicing.[54]

The masculine love that is cut off from feminine love, however, is as imperfect as the feminine love that is separated from masculine love. Life hardly survives in the bitter cold battlefield, but it can easily be corrupted in the dark swamp. To become a whole, healthy, and true love, both the masculine and feminine elements of love ought to be integrated. Only when the sacred marriage between the principles of masculine and feminine, in Jung's language, is achieved in one's psyche, can the philosophy of "dan" or the "violence of love" be substantiated into a true reality

The unification of opposite sexual components is the very process that transpired during Kim's struggle. His later works show that his concern for the preservation and nurturing of life grew to become even greater than his early concern for the fight for justice. With this newly emerged concern he emphasizes more of the aspects of "relatedness," "flexibility," "wholeness," "kindness," and "diversity of life."[55] The spiritual encounter between persons through dialogue is as important as the fight against the oppressor. His image is transformed from the figure of the heroic fighter to that of the caring mother. The liberation of women has been one of his prominent concerns since 1984, which shows the integration of the feminine element into Kim's personality.[56]

Seen in the light of later developments in Kim's psychic reality, the practice of "dan" should be understood as one element in the dynamic process of the transformation of *han* than as the sole soteriology of *han*. At a certain stage of the process, "dan" can become a negative element obstructing the transformation. Just as the masculine "dan" is a crucial element to break through the wall of the prison of *han* and to free its energy, the feminine element is also crucial to restrain the violent energy of *han* and to transform it into life energy. This feminine love is called "jeong" in the Korean language which, when it lacks the masculine element of "dan," becomes the masochistic, self-inflicted pain of sorrow; but when it is integrated with the liberated masculine aggression, becomes the power of love that creates and nurtures life and beauty as well as justice.

3. Toward a Theology of Healing

The late Professor Nam-dong Suh, the main initiator of Minjung Theology, hoped that Minjung Theology would become a theology of *han*.[57] His hope is still alive in the continuing efforts of Minjung theologians, and of those who cherish Minjung Theology and try to contribute to it from diverse perspectives. This hope is extended to the concern for a theology of healing of *han*.

When the pioneering Minjung theologians discovered the ore of *han*, the root of Korean culture and spirituality, their experience was similar to that of the proverbial farmer who came upon buried treasure hidden in a field and, in his excitement, sold everything to buy that field. They needed tools to analyze and interpret the newly found treasure. Thus they listened to Chi-ha Kim who suggested the use of liberation Theology for a hermeneutical tool in analyzing and interpreting *han*.

> First of all, I am convinced that . . . in the tradition of tenacious resistance and revolution of Korean *minjung* exists an ore of gold from which the principle of unification of God and revolution as a new principle of human liberation, and which worth to represent to the world, especially to the Third-world. When this ore is trimmed off with the chisel of Liberation Theology, the 'Missio Dei' will bring about a miracle in the tradition of the Korean *minjung*'s struggle.[58]

Minjung theologians accepted this suggestion and attempted to use the hermeneutics of Latin American Liberation Theology as the main model for the exploration of the reality of *han*. Because their emphasis was on the social, political, and economic aspects, the psychological and spiritual aspects have remain unexplored. The next step for Minjung Theology, then, is to take seriously this unexplored part of *han*. This task requires hermeneutics other than that of Liberation Theology to delve into the depths of the *han* reality. As a body of knowledge about the human mind depth psychology can be used as an efficient tool for Minjung Theology.

The Korean traditional understanding of the two categories of "wonhan" and "jeong-han" acquires scientific validation through its correspondence to the knowledge of psycho-analysis, specifically to Melanie Klein's theories of the paranoid-schizoid position and the depressive position. In alliance with the theoretical development in psychoanalysis which distinguishes the schizoid position from the paranoid position, the third type of *han*, "huhan," can be distinguished as one of the three categories of *han*. The discernment of the three types of *han* and the different qualities of their inner natures can be used as indispensable landmarks in the territory of *han* to avoid getting lost in that strange land. The lack of discernment of the different types of *han* is responsible for the unproductive debates between advocates of "jeong-han" and those of "wonhan" in the field of Korean literature as well as Korean culture in general. When the "wonhan" advocates oppose the "jeong-han," they are in fact advocating the mature "jeong-han" that can utilize aggression creatively, as opposed to the premature "jeong-han" with its masochistic uses of aggression and sentimental love. Likewise, when the "jeong-han" advocates oppose "wonhan," they are not opposing the progressive power of *han* but the primitive, destructive impulse of "wonhan." With its predominant feeling of emptiness, "huhan" poses a serious social problem. People of "huhan" suffer boredom, dullness, futility, and meaninglessness in their everyday lives. As a desperate effort to escape from the psychological predicament they often find solution in devoting themselves to a great social cause or ideology and thus become members of a collective social force. The collective social force rooted in "huhan" expresses itself in violent destructive social activities, because "huhan" by its nature seeks out destruction. People of "huhan" are nihilists who value nothing in themselves and society, though they worship a great social cause or ideology expressed in their slogans and statements.

Beneath the surface, however, they are seeking excitement and a sense of being real, which they may feel in those moments of collective confrontation with opposing social forces. It is an illusion to build a humane, healthy society upon "huhan" type social activities, no matter how beautiful their slogans and statements. At the center of these "huhan" people exists an empty shell in which no value, beauty, authentic feeling, or hope can be contained. Therefore, a discernment is needed to distinguish between social activities that are based on genuine and healthy personal values, and those that are based on false, sick and nihilistic tendencies of destruction. The lack of discernment of the categories of *han* is responsible for the one-sided romanticization of *han* in Minjung Theology, in which symbols arising from are used indiscriminately as political metaphor for the purpose of bringing about social change, as is shown in the deification of Tae-il Chun's self-immolation. According to the insights of analytical psychology initiated by Carl G. Jung, the resolution of *han* can be achieved by the process of transformation of personality. The journey of *han* is equated with the journey of realization of one's true self in life. Furthermore, in the resolution of *han*, one goes beyond the aim of the individual self to devoted service to the Self who comes from the side of the "beyond" in the image of gods (or archetypes in Jung's terms). The illumination of nature and function of both the shell part of the complex and its core, which is illustrated through the symbolic interpretation of the "Barikongjoo" myth and the shaman initiation ritual, extends the scope of the understanding of *han* in Korean culture in general and in Minjung Theology in particular. In understanding *han* using Jung's insights, the importance of individuation as a necessary step toward healthy individuals and society is highlighted. Through the individuation process the healing of *han* of both individuals and society can take place. With the progress of the individuation process one is liberated from the grip of negative complexes and becomes able to use the dammed up energies more freely and constructively for a meaningful individual life as well as for a better communal life. As a result of the psychological and spiritual journey of the individuation process, individuals find their meaningful purpose in life in relation to themselves, others, and God and finally realize their life's work through fulfilling their vocations. Individuation is the best and surest way to release a society from the spell of "wonhan," "huhan," or immature "jeong-han" type social problems, because it is the very process through which the inner source of values, creative impulses, and hope is restored and consolidated at the center of one's being.

The reality of the *han* of *minjung* demands that Minjung Theology be a theology of healing, which not only listens to the cries and the sighs of suffering *minjung*, but also heals their inner wounds of *han*. Minjung Theology, which started as a theology of the cry of the suffering *minjung*, tried to locate the source of that cry in the unjust and oppressive social reality. It was a significant contribution to the service of *minjung*. The reality of *han*, however, calls our attention to the source of the cry located in the heart of *minjung* themselves. Now Minjung Theology is invited to a practice of healing that wipes the tears from the eyes of *minjung* and heals the wounds in their hearts. Slogans and statements about the *han* cannot heal the wounds of *han*. What brings forth healing is love that is strong and spacious enough to contain the aggression of the wounded hearts so that the healing process can start. With this practice of healing, Minjung Theology can truly serve *minjung* and the True God, the God of love and justice.

CHAPTER VII

CONCLUSION

In Korean culture *han* is understood as series of feelings. In this study it is shown that the source of these feelings is rooted in one's personality. This root of *han* in personality has its origin in the inner wounds that occurred in the early days of infant life. When the original wounds of the baby are fixated and remain in the deeper realm of the psyche without being healed, they become the base of *han* in the personality of that individual. The base of *han* in personality consists fundamentally of two different structures--"wonhan" and "jeong-han." The inner dynamics of these two structures of *han* are, in their nature, equivalent to those of Melanie Klein's two positions--paranoid-schizoid position and depressive position. Besides the two basic categories of *han*, a third category of *han*, "huhan," with its characteristic feeling of emptiness, is accorded its own existence. This additional categorization may contribute to further clarity in understanding *han* phenomena, or at least may reduce some confusion involved in understanding *han*. These three basic types of *han* are the sources of suffering.

Han, however, is not just source of suffering, but also the source of creativity and energy to proceed in the process of the transformation of the personality. It is the emotional basis for the establishment of the humane society based on justice and love. The differentiation of the quality of *han* is thus crucial. Because the answer to the question whether a certain *han* brings forth constructive results or destructive results to the individuals and society depends upon the quality of the *han*. If the *han* is predominantly of hate and aggression unmodified with love, it can hardly create any goodness in one's personality or in society.

With its increased capacities of discernment, Minjung Theology can discern the authentic religious symbols of the Korean people. This is meaningful for two purposes; to bridge the gap between Korean indigenous religious symbols and those of Christianity, and to avoid the confusion of religious syncretism. Korean Christianity seems lost contact with the depths of the Korean mind by its exclusive attitude toward Korean indigenous religious symbols. For instance, the dream images that Korean Christians experience are predominantly tinctured with Korean Shamanism, which they regard as contemptible on a conscious level. This phenomenon suggests that their psyche is in a state of division. Their consciousness belongs to Christianity while unconscious belongs to Shamanism. Then the Christian symbols become substitutes for the Shamanistic symbols. Many Korean Christians resort to shamanistic practices for their spiritual resources while using Christian terms and formalities. As a result, they cannot utilize the powerful energy that they experience in their religious practices as resources for their conscious, ethical, and socio-political lives. The energy originating in the unconscious cannot be channeled into consciousness because the newly adopted symbols, grown in the soil of different culture and history, cannot translate the primordial images of the psyche into meaningful symbolic language. This is why religious syncretism is undesirable. The discernment of authentic Korean religious symbols does not lead to a fixation with nationalistic religious symbols, but to the liberation from fixation on any religious symbol system. There may be differences in color, shape, or intensity among those symbolic images, but the discernment of these differences can create a space in which we can transcend the visible differences of the symbols and become able to freely appreciate the truth of our being and of God in an authentic way. This creative inner space should become the locus of Minjung Theology in the course of healing the inner wounds of the Korean people.

The importance of the process of the transformation of the symbols of *han* is emphasized, especially in the study of the symbolism of *han* in Korean Shamanism. The transformation of the symbolism of *han* in Korean Shamanism opens the realm of the mystery of our being beyond our personal experience in time and history. The reality of *han* opens our eyes to the world of collective unconscious, where we find the unique meaning of our life and fulfill it in our personality as well as in the service of the society and God.

The End.

NOTES

Chapter I

1. Eun Ko, "Introspection on *Han*," *The Sound of My Inner Wave* (Seoul: Nanam, 1987), 384.

2. Kosuke Koyama, "Building the House by Righteousness: The Ecumenical Horizon of Minjung Theology," *An Emerging Theology in the World Perspective: Commentary on Korean Minjung Theology*, ed. Jung Yong Lee (Mystic, Connecticut: Twenty Third Publications, 1988), 142.

3. Yul-kyu Kim, *The Ore of Han and the Stream of Won* (Seoul: Joowoo, 1981), 15.

4. Carl G. Jung, *The Archetypes and the Collective Unconscious* C.W. vol. 9.1, 2nd ed. (Princeton: Princeton University Press, 1968), 42-43.

5. This term used in this study includes both psychoanalytical and analytical psychology. Depth psychology, pioneered by Sigmund Freud, is a branch of psychology exploring both the conscious and the unconscious of human mind. Analytical psychology, founded by Carl G. Jung, approaches the unconscious differently in many ways from that of Freud, calling serious attention to the intrinsic value of unconscious, which should not be placed under the control of the consciousness.

6. The psychology of Carl G. Jung has obtained an honorable stance among Korean scholars across the different fields of study such as psychiatry, religion, folk study, etc., whereas that of Melanie Klein has hardly been introduced to Korean academic society. Several of Jung's book are translated into Korean whereas none of Klein's major articles are translated into Korean.

7. Carl G. Jung, "The Synthetic or Constructive Method," trans. R. F. C. Hull, *Two Essays on Analytical Psychology* (Princeton: Princeton University Press, 1972).

8. For similarities of Klein and Jung see Ann B. Ulanov's article "A Shared Space, Jung and Others," *Quadrant*, Journal of the C. G. Jung Foundation for Analytical Psychology, Spring 1985, vol.18, No.1.

Chapter II

1. Kyu-tae Lee, *The History of Korean Folklore* (Seoul: Hyuneumsa, 1983), 93-104.

2. Sigmund Freud, *Inhibitions, Symptoms and Anxiety* (1926) trans. Alix Strachey, revised and ed. James Strachey (New York: W.W.Norton & Company, 1959), 87. Freud in this writing revised his theory of anxiety, approaching it from a different vantage point. Instead of the economy of libido theory, he focused on the ego as the sole seat of anxiety. Anxiety is a signal from the ego concerning the danger that can come from the id, external reality, or the super-ego. The magnitude of danger is measured in the ego's experiences of helplessness in the face of that danger, whether physical or psychical. In doing this, the ego is guided by actual past experiences of helplessness which had resulted in traumatic situations. Anxiety is the original reaction to helplessness during the trauma, and it is reproduced later in the danger situation to act as a signal that danger is present. Freud distinguishes neurotic anxiety from realistic anxiety. Realistic anxiety is anxiety about a known danger, but neurotic anxiety is caused by an unknown danger and comes from the pressure of instinct.

The concept of neurotic anxiety in Freud's later theory can be related to the concept of han. Anxiety is one of the components of han, whose source is hidden, but exists in the traumatic situation of the real experience of helplessness. Just as a surplus of anxiety betrays the existence of trauma in an afflicted person, any surplus of han betrays the existence of trauma in an individual.

3. For Jung, the function of sexual instinct is to facilitate the process of realization of the self. C. G. Jung, "Individuation," *Two Essays on Analytical Psychology* (Princeton: Princeton University Press, 1953).

4. Victor E. Frankl, *Man's Search for the Meaning* (New York: Pocket Books, 1959).

5. Yul-kyu Kim, *The Ore of Han and The Stream of Won*, 23.

6. Ibid., 17-20.

7. Ibid., 22.

8. Ibid., 21, 26.

9. Ibid., 21, 28.

10. Ibid., 22.

11. Ibid., 24-25.

12. A Korean peasant revolution occurred in the 18th century as the peasants reacted to the corrupt government officials' extreme oppression. The peasants attempted to establish a new social reality under the guidance of the teachings of Tonghak Religion, founded by Je-woo Choi, whose teaching was "to treat human being like the heaven."

13. Yul-kyu Kim's view on the nature han is generally consistent with this author's, except that he does not give a coherent explanation about the relationships between "wonhan" and "jeong-han."

14. Young-sook Kim Harvey, "An Interpretation: "sinbyung" as a pathway out of impasse," *The Six Korean Women* (St. Paul, Minnesota: West Publishing Co., 1979), 240.

15. Ibid., 237.

16. Tae-gon Kim, *A Study of Korean Shamanism* (Seoul: Jipmoondang, 1981), 247.

17. Young-sook Kim Harvey provides a description of a Korean shaman who converted to Christianity. The deaconess Chang, the former shaman, had to go through tremendous mental and psychosomatic affliction during the transitional period. The symptoms were essentially the same as with the traditional "sinbyung," except this time she experienced a far more horrifying vision of fighting between the forces of the Devil and Jesus Christ, and her interpretation was different. In this case, she interpreted it as a necessary step to achieve the experience of the Holy Ghost. Young-sook Kim Harvey, Ibid., 209.

Based on Kim Harvey's report, Kwang-sun Suh claims that in the Korean church the spirit possession of shamanism has been transferred to faith in the Holy Ghost. "Shamanism: the religion of Han," *Essays on Korean Heritage and Christianity* (Princeton Junction, N.J.: AKCS Publication, 1984), 83.

18. Tae-gon Kim, Ibid., 257-259.

19. Among the modern writers who deal with the theme of han Yul-kyu Kim includes Moon-ku Lee, Woo-ahm Paik, Ji-hoon Cho, Sowol Kim, Jung-joo Suh, Mok-wol Park, Sang Yi, Dong-joo Yoon, Jung-rae Cho, Seung-won Han, Chung-joon Lee, Yoon-suk Huh, Suk-young Hwang, and Sang-kook Chun. Yul-kyu Kim, *The Ore of Han and the Stream of Won.*

20. Hun-uoung Im, "The Literature of Han and the Consciousness of Minjung," *Today's Book* (Seoul: Hangilsa, 1984), 87-92.

21. Eun Ko, "Introspection on *Han*," *The Voice of My Wave* (Seoul: Nanam, 1987), 375-407.

22. Hun-yung Im, Ibid., 106-109.

23. Ibid., 110.

24. Bou-yong Rhie, "Illness and Healing in the Three Kingdoms Period," *Korea Journal* (December, 1981), 7.

25. Bou-yong Rhie, "Dealing with Evil in Korean Fairytales," *Korea Journal* (January, 1980), 20.

26. Ibid., 26.

27. Ibid., 23.

28. Ibid., 20.

29. Ibid., 21.

30. Ibid.

31. Ibid., 21-22.

32. Ibid., 21.

33. Ibid., 25.

34. Bou-yong Rhie, "The Relationship Between Death and Han," *The Lost Shadow* (Seoul: Jungwoosa, 1983), 153.

35. Including Young-sook Kim Harvey and Tae-gon Kim.

36. Kwang-il Kim, "Psychoanalysis of Sinbyung," *Psychoanalysis of the Korean Traditional Culture* (Seoul: Siensa, 1984), 205.

37. Ibid., 206-209.

38. Ibid., 209-210.

39. Ibid., 210-212.

40. Ibid., 212-213.

41. Ibid., 213-215.

42. Ibid., 215-216.

43. Ibid., 216-219.

44. Ibid., 219,220.

45. Ibid., 223-224.

46. Ibid., 221.

47. Ibid., 223.

48. Yul-kyu Kim, *The Ore of Han and the Stream of Won.* 23.

Chapter III

1. Phyllis Grosskurth, *Melanie Klein: Her World and Her Work* (Cambridge, MA: Harvard University Press, 1987).

2. Hanna Segal, "Melanie Klein: The Person and Her Work," *Melanie Klein* (New York: Viking Press, 1979), 169.

3. Sigmund Freud, "Analysis of a Phobia in a Five-Year-Old Boy" (1909), S.E. 10 (London: The Hogarth Press: 1955), 5-146.

4. Except some work by Hermine von Hug-Hellmuth (1871-1924) and Anna Freud soon after in Vienna. Paul Roazen, *Freud and His Followers* (New York: Alfred A. Knopf, Inc., 1971), 442-443.

5. Melanie Klein, "The Psychological Foundations" (1926), *The Psycho-Analysis of Children* (Seymour Lawrence: Delacorte, 1975), 7.

6. Susan Isaacs, "The Nature and Function of Phantasy," *Developments in Psycho-Analysis*, 83. Quoted from Hanna Segal, 97.

7. Melanie Klein, "The Technique of Early Analysis" (1926), *The Psycho-Analysis of Children*, 16.

8. Melanie Klein, "The Psychological Foundations" (1926), 3-7.

9. Melanie Klein, "The Technique of Early Analysis" (1932), *The Psycho-Analysis of Children*, 29.

10. Melanie Klein, "Personification in the Play of Children" (1929), *Love, Guilt and Reparation & Other Works* (New York: Delta, 1975), 201-205.

11. Melanie Klein was basically following Freud's frame of child development: oral, anal, phallic, genital and sexual.

12. Melanie Klein, "The Thoery of Anxiety and Guilt" (1948), *Envy and Gratitude & Other Works* (New York: Free Press, 1984), 29.

13. Ibid., 28-30.

14. Ibid., 31-33.

15. Melanie Klein, "Development of Conscious in the Child" (1933), *Love, Guilt and Reparation*, 251.

16. Melanie Klein thinks that a sufficient quantity of anxiety is the necessary basis for an abundance of symbol-formation and of phantasy. This symbol-formation is the foundation of all sublimation and of every talent only if an adequate capacity on the part of the ego to tolerate anxiety is allowed. Melanie Klein, "Symbol-Formation in Ego Development" (1938), *Love, Guilt and Reparation*, 220-221.

17. Melanie Klein, "The Theory of Anxiety and Guilt" (1948), *Envy and Gratitude & Other Works*, 31.

18. This transition occurs in the second quarter of the child's first year. Melanie Klein, "A Contribution to the Psychogenesis of Manic-Depressive States" (1935), *Love, Guilt and Other Works*, 264-267.

19. Melanie Klein, "The Theory of Anxiety and Guilt," 34.

20. Melanie Klein, "A Contribution to Psychogenesis of Manic-Depressive States," 270.

21. Melanie Klein, "Love, Guilt and Reparation" (1937), *Love Guilt and Reparation*, 326, 327.

22. Melanie Klein, "Our Adult World and Its Roots in Infancy" (1959), *Envy and Gratitude & Other Works*, 255.

23. Melanie Klein, "The Importance of Symbol-Formation in the Development of the Ego" (1930), *Love Guilt and Raparation*, 220-222.

24. Melanie Klein, "A Contribution to the Psychogenesis of the Manic-Depressive States," 288.

25. Cf. Chapter II.

26. Yul-kyu Kim, *The Ore of Han and the Stream of Won* (Seoul; Joowoosa, 1981), 21.

27. Yul-kyu Kim simply describes that both masochism and sadism operate in han without explaining the relationship between them. Ibid., 22.

28. Hanna Segal, *Melanie Klein*, 126.

29. This central insight came from Freud and Abraham. Freud had assumed that the infant's first relation was to the breast. And Abraham observed the importance of the relation to part objects such as breast or feces. Hanna Segal, *Melanie Klein*, 45.

30. Melanie Klein, "Notes on Some Schizoid Mechanisms" (1946), *Envy and Gratitude & Other Works*, 8-9.

31. Ibid.

32. Ibid., 7.

33. Melanie Klein, "The Importance of Symbol-Formation in the Development of the Ego" (1930), *Love, Guilt and Reparation*, 221-231.

34. Hanna Segal, Melanie Klein, 120.

35. Melanie Klein, "On Identification " (1955), *Envy and Gratitude & Other Works*, 143-144.

36. Melanie Klein, "Notes on Some Schizoid Mechanisms," 9.

37. Melanie Klein, "The Emotional Life of the Infant" (1952), *Envy and Gratitude & Other Works*, 73.

38. Melanie Klein, "Notes on Some Schizoid Mechanisms," 9-13.

39. Melanie Klein, Ibid., 11.

40. Melanie Klein, "The Emotional Life of the Infant" (1952), *Envy and Gratitude & Other Works* (New York: The Free Press, 1984), 69.

41. In Klein's view fixation is produced by aggression and anxiety whereas in Freud's view it is produced by frustration. Hanna segal, *Melanie Klein*, 106-107.

42. Hanna Segal, *Melanie Klein*, 122.

43. Phyllis Grosskurth, *Melanie Klein: Her World and Her Work*, 216.

44. Melanie Klein, "A Contribution to the Psychogenesis of Manic-Depressive States," 286-288.

45. Ibid., 270.

46. Melanie Klein, "Mourning and Its Position to Manic-Derpessive States" (1940), 352-354.

47. Hanna Segal, "The Depressive Position," *Introduction to the Work of*

Melanie Klein (New York: Basic Books, 1964), 70.

48. Freud finds that in mourning the libido gets gradually detached from the lost object and is free for investment in a new object. By contrast, in melancholia the object is introjected and the libido is turned inward. Sigmund Freud, "Mourning and Melancholia" (1917), *S.E.* 14 (London: The Hogarth Press, 1955), 245-246.

49. Hanna Segal, "Manic Defenses," *Introduction to the Work of Melanie Klein*, 83-84.

50. Melanie Klein, "A Contribution to Psychogenesis of Manic-Depressive States," 276.

51. Hanna Segal, "Reparation," 92-102.

52. Melanie Klein, "The Oedipus Complex in the Light of Early Anxieties" (1945), *Love, Guilt and Reparation & Other Works*, 397.

53. Melanie Klein, "Infantile Anxiety Situations Reflected in a Work of Art and in the Creative Impulse" (1929), 214-218.

54. Melanie Klein, "On Identification" (1955), *Envy and Gratitude & Other Works*, 144.

55. Hanna Segal, Melanie Klein, 138.

56. A Korean indigenous religion founded by Jeung-san Kang, whose main teaching was "hae-won," the resolution of "wonhan."

57. Jung-rip Lee, *Jeungsan Thought*, vol.3. Quoted from "Literature of Han and Consciousness of People," Hun-young Im, *Books Today* (Seoul: Hangilsa, 1984), 91.

58. Yul-Kyu Kim, *The Ore of Han and the Stream of Won*, 23.

59. Kwang-il Kim, "A Psycho-Analysis of Sinbyung," *A Psychoanalysis of Korean Shamanism* (Seoul: Siensa, 1984), 204-225.

60. Tae-gon Kim, *A Study of Korean Shamanism* (Seoul: Jipmoondang, 1981), 258-259.

61. Melanie Klein, "Notes on Some Schizoid Mechanisms," *Envy and Gratitude & Other Works*, 13-15.

62. Harry Guntrip, Schizoid Phenomena, *Object Relations and the Self* (New York: International University Press, 1969), 57.

63. Eun Ko, *The Sound of My Wave* (Seoul: Nanam, 1987), 398.

64. The importance of the mother's role in the formation of the core is most eloquently emphasized in the study of D. W. Winnicott. D. W. Winnicott, "The Theory of the Parent-infant Relationship" (1960), "Ego Distortion in terms of True and False Self" (1969), *The Maturational Processes and the Facilitating Environment* (New York: International University Press, 1965). "Transitional Object and Transitional Phenomena" (1953), "Mirror-role of Mother and Family in Child Development" (1967), *Playing and Reality* (London: Tavistock Publication Ltd., 1971). "The Mother's Contribution to Society" (1957), *Home is Where We Start*

From (New York & London: W.W.Norton & Company, 1986).

65. Melanie Klein, "Envy an Gratitude" (1957), *Envy and Gratitude and Other Works* (New York: The Free Press, 1984), 179-180.

66. Hanna Segal, Melanie Klein, 144-146.

67. Melanie Klein, "Love, Guilt and Reparation" (1937), *Love, Guilt and Reparation*, 322-324.

68. Envy is the only psychological factor among them while the rest are external, political, economic ones. Yul-kyu Kim, The Ore of Han and the Stream of Won, 23.

69. The psychological and theological meanings of envy in the story of Cinderella--a Western version of "Kongjui-Patjui"--are investigated by Ann and Barry Ulanov in their book, *Cinderella & Her Sisters: The Envied and The Envying* (Philadelphia: The Westminster Press, 1983).

70. Woon-sik Choi, "A Study of the Step-mother Folklore," *Korean Folk Customs* (Seoul: Kyunghee University, 1986), 11-12.

Chapter IV

1. The Yi dynasty lasted about five hundred years (1392-1905 A.D.).

2. The Committee of National History Publication, *The History of Korea* vol. 9 (Seoul: Tamgoodang, 1974), 96-100.

3. Ibid., 102.

4. The Committee of National History Publication, *The History of Korea*, vol.12 (Seoul: Tamgoodang, 1978), 169-179.

5. Ibid.

6. Ibid.

7. The Korean History Association, *The Korean History in Story Telling* (Seoul: Chungah Press, 1987), 295-300.

8. Sejo was the seventh king of the Yi dynasty who became king by killing the young Danjong, the sixth king.

9. Ibid., 301.

10. Ibid., 303-307.

11. The Committee of National History Publication, *The History of Korea*, vol.12, 169-179.

12. Ibid.

13. Ibid.

14. Ibid.

15. Dong-shik Ryu, *The History and Structure of the Korean Shamanism* (Seoul: Yonsei University Press, 1975), 205-207.

16. The Korean History Association, *The Korean History in Story Telling*, 307-313.

17. The Committee of National History Publication, *The History of Korea* vol.12, 3.

18. The Korean History Association, The Korean History in Story Telling, 306-307.

19. Ibid., 304-305.

20. The Korean History Association, *Korean History in Story Telling*, 300.

21. The National Culture Association, *Yun-Ryu-Sil-Ki-Sul*, (Seoul: Kwangmyungsa, 1966), 96.

22. Dong-shik Ryu, *The History and Structure of the Korean Shamanism*, 206.

23. The Committee of National History Publication, *The History of Korea* vol.12, 169-179.

24. The Korean History Association, *The Korean History in Story Telling*, 298.

25. Phyllis Grosskurth, *Melanie Klein: Her World and Her Work* (Cambridge, MA: Harvard University Press, 1987), 415.

26. Sowol obtained a national nickname among Korean people, "the poet of *han*." Won-sup Lee, *The Poems of Sowol* (Seoul: Hyunamsa, 1973), 91.

27. Translated by the author. Yul-kyu Kim, *The Ore of Han and Stream of Won* (Seoul:joowoo, 1981), 31.

28. Translated by the author. Yul-kyu Kim, *The Ore of Han and the Stream of Won*, 90.

29. Translated by the author. Won-sup Lee, *The Poems of Sowol*, 56.

30. Ibid.

31. Translated by the author. Ibid., 114.

32. Translated by the author.

33. Cf. Chapter II.

34. Translated by Chang-soo Ko. *Korea's Best Loved Poems* (Seoul: Hanrim, 1974), 80.

35. A cuckoo family bird.

36. An onomatopoeia of the cuckoo.

37. Translated by the author. Won-sup Lee, *The Poems of Sowol*, 204.

38. A Korean fairytale similar to the Cinderella story. Cf. Chapter III.

39. Translated by Chang-soo Ko. *Korea's Best Loved Poems*, 37.

40. About a two and half mile distance.

41. Melanie Klein, "On the Theory of Anxiety and Guilt" (1948), *Envy and*

Gratitude & Other Works (New York: Free Press, 1975), 34.

    42. Ibid., 37.

    43. Man-young Jang, "Sowol Kim," *The Great People of Korea* (Seoul: Bahgwoosa, 1972), ed. The Publication Committee of the Great People of Korea, 278.

    44. Mok-wol Park, *The Features of the Great People in Korea* (Seoul: Shingoo Moonhwasa, 1965), ed. Hee-sung Lee and Others, 444.

    45. Man-young Jang, "Sowol Kim," *The Great People of Korea*, 279.

    46. Eun Ko was a member of the Central Committee for the National Democracy Affiliation, the largest organization of the socio-political and cultural movement in Korea in those days. The Minjung movement was a Korean people's movement which emerged during the struggle for democracy and human rights against the military dictatorship of the 1970s and 1980s.

    47. Eun Ko, *Being Transformed, Where Shall We Meet?* (Seoul: Joongang Press, 1971), 11.

    48. Ibid., 34, 99, 266.

    49. Ibid., 191.

    50. Ibid., 104.

    51. Ibid., 134, 288.

    52. Ibid., 14.

    53. Ibid., 255.

    54. Ibid., 85-87.

    55. Ibid., 319-320.

    56. Ibid., 115-116.

    57. Ibid., 178.

    58. Ibid., 178.

    59. Ibid., 131-132, 263-264.

    60. Ibid., 305, 306.

    61. Ibid., 125, 311.

    62. The Korean word "dangshin" means thou, darling, sweetheart, or you.

    63. Ibid., 42, 98.

    64. Ibid., 113, 126-128, 209, 288.

    65. Ibid., 43, 209.

    66. Ibid., 131-133.

    67. Ibid., 343.

    68. Ibid., 113.

    69. Ibid., 255.

    70. Ibid., 323, 324.

    71. Ibid., 343.

    72. Melanie Klein, *Love, Guilt and Reparation* (New York: Dell Publishing

Co., Inc., 1975), 276. Guntrip distinguishes the difference between the depressive suicide and schizoid suicide as follows;

> Whereas in depressive suicide the driving force is anger, aggression, hate, and a destructive impulse aimed at the self to divert it from the hated love-object, i.e. self-murder, schizoid suicide is at bottom a longing to escape from a situation that one just does not feel strong enough to cope with, so as in some sense to return to the womb and be born later with a second chance to live. Harry Guntrip, *Schizoid Phenomena, Object Relations and the Self* (New York; International University Press, 1969), 218.

73. Eun Ko, *The Son of Red Soil; My Childhood* (Seoul; Hangilsa, 1986), 7.

74. Ibid., 16.

75. Ibid., 38.

76. Ibid., Foreword.

77. Winnicott claims that the aetiology of the schizoid problem should be found in an environmental failure rather than in instinctual forces in the child. For him, the infant-mother relationship is more important than the early mechanisms of ego-defense organized against the id-impulse, although of course these two aspects overlap. He understands the schizoid personality problem in relation to the development of the false self and the true self. The false self is the healthy part of the personality when it serves the function of defense of the healthy, true self. With the true self hidden inside, however, withdrawn and unable to unfold its potentiality, the personality is made out of a series of defenses whose main function is to comply with the environment and to protect the hidden true self. With a "good-enough mother," who does not have to be perfect but who is physically and emotionally healthy enough to be in tune with the physical and emotional needs of the baby, the baby has a chance to develop its own true self. D. W. Winnicott, *The Maturation Processes and the Facilitating Environment* (New York; International Universities Press Inc., 1965), 140-152.

78. Eun Ko, *For Disillusionment* (Seoul: Mineumsa, 1976), 84.

79. Eun Ko, *The Peak of the Wind* (Seoul: Nanam, 1987), 39-50.

80. Eun Ko, *For Disillusionment*, 146.

81. Ibid., 154.

82. Eun Ko, *The Son of Red Soil*, 151.

83. Eun Ko, *The Peak of Wind*, 17.

84. Eun Ko, *The Sound of My Wave*, 277-371.

85. Eun Ko, *The Son of Red Soil*, 17.

86. These are the names of four rivers in Korea.

87. These are well respected Korean patriots who devoted their lives for the

Korean people.

88. Eun Ko, *The Peak of the Wind*, 118.

89. Ibid., 119.

90. Eun Ko, *Being Transformed, Where Shall We Meet?*, 85.

91. Ibid., 305.

92. David Holbrook, *Education, Nihilism & Survival* (London: Darton, Longman & Todd Ltd., 1977), 24-25.

93. Eun Ko, *The Sound of My Wave*, 398, 401-408.

Chapter V

1. Dong-sik Ryu, *The History and the Structure of Korean Shamanism* (Seoul: Yonsei University Press, 1975), 288-291.

2. Ibid., 346.

3. Minjung theologians, especially Nam-dong Suh and Kwang-sun Suh made this point clear in their works. *Minjung Theology*, ed. Kim Yong Bock (Singapore: The Commission on Theological Concerns, 1981).

4. The analysis of "Sinbyung" is done by Kwang-il Kim. Cf. Chapter II.

5. Carl G. Jung, "The Synthetic or Constructive Method," *Two Essays on Analytic Psychology*, Paperback edition (Princeton: Princeton University Press, 1972), 80-89.

6. Ann Belford Ulanov, *The Feminine in Jungian Psychology and in Christian Theology* (Evanston: Northwestern University Press, 1971), 21.

7. Ibid., 22.

8. Dong-sik Ryu, *The History and Structure of the Korean Shamanism* (Seoul: Yonsei University Press, 1975), 293-294.

9. Kwang-sun Suh, "Shamanism: The Religion of han," *Essays on the Korean Heritage and Christianity*, ed. Sang-hyun Lee (Princeton: AKCS, 1984), 68.

10. Tae-gon Kim, *A Study of Korean Shamanism* (Seoul: Jipmoondang, 1981), 243.

11. Ibid., 162-193.

12. Kwang-il Kim, *The Psychoanalysis of the Korean Traditional Culture* (Seoul: Siensa, 1984), 40-41.

13. This story is excerpted from Tae-gon Kim's collection and translated by the author. Tae-gon Kim, *The Myths of Korean Shamanism* (Seoul: Jipmoondang, 1985), 47-81.

14. In some other versions she is called "Berideki" or "Birideki." Ibid., 32, 47, 57.

15. Young-sook Kim Harvey, "Women and Family in Traditional Korea," *Six Korean Women* (New York: West Publishing Company, 1979), 263-265.

16. Ann Belford Ulanov, *The Feminine in Jungian Psychology and in Christian Theology* (Evanston: Northwestern University Press, 1971), 158.

17. Alice Miller, *The Prisoners of Childhood*, Trans. Ruth Ward (New York: Basic Books, Inc., Publishers), 100.

18. Tae-gon Kim Provides four life histories of shamans including one male shaman. Among them two women shamans recall they were born as unwanted girl babies. *The Study of Korean Shamanism*, 247-259.

19. Kwang-sun Suh, *Essays on Korean Heritage and Christianity*, 84.

20. Bou-yong Rhie, *Analytical Psychology* (Seoul: Iljogak, 1987), 317.

21. Kwang-sun Suh, *Essays on the Korean Heritage and Christianity*, 69.

22. Edward F. Edinger, *Outline of Analytical Psychology, 11.*

23. Jolande Jacobi, *The Psychology of Jung*, trans. Ralph Manheim (New York: Pantheon, 1959), 8-9.

24. Carl G. Jung, *C. G. Jung*, C.W. vol.8, trans. R.F.C. Hull, *The Structure and Dynamics of the Psyche* (Princeton: Princeton University Press, 1960), 96.

25. Carl G. Jung *C. G. Jung*, C.W. vol.5, trans. R.F.C. Hull, *Symbols of Transformation* (Princeton: Princeton University Press, 1967), 305.

26. Ann Belford Ulanov, "Our Search for Paternal Roots: Jungian Perspectives on Fathering," *Fathering* ed. Edward V. Stein (Nashville: Abingdon, 1977).

27. Dong-sik Lee, *The Identity of Korean People and Tao* (Seoul: Iljisa, 1974), 161.

28. Marie-Louise von Franz, *Alchemy* (Toronto, Canada: Inner City Books, 1980), 29.

29. Tae-gon Kim, *The Myths of Korean Shamanism*, 66.

30. Ibid., 65.

31. Carl G. Jung, C. G. Jung, C.W. vol.5, *Symbols of Transformation*, 330.

32. Cf, Chapter IV.

33. Edward F. Edinger, *Outline of Analytic Psychology*, 13.

34. Ann Belford Ulanov, *The Feminine in Jungian Psychology and in Christian Theology*, 33.

35. Ann Belford Ulanov, "The Psychological Reality of the Demonic," *Picturing God* (New York: Cowley Publication, 1986), 131.

36. A term later adopted by Jung to avoid the confusion of the word "collective" with collectivity.

37. Ann Belford Ulanov, *The Feminine in Jungian Psychology and in Christian Theology*, 35-36.

38. Ibid., 41.

39. Ibid., 32.

40. Tae-gon Kim, *The Myths of Korean Shamanism*. 73.

41. J. E. Cirlot, *A Dictionary of Symbols*, trans. Jack Sage (New York: Philosophical Library, 1962).

42. Bou-yong Rhie, *Analytical Psychology*, 102.

43. Ann Belford Ulanov, *The Feminine in Jungian Psychology and In Christian Theology*, 63.

44. Bou-yong Rhie, *Analytical Psychology*, 102.

45. Marie-Louise von Franz, *Alchemy*, 158.

46. The names of the six Buddhas cited in the story are; Virozona, Wonmangbishinosana, Shakymuni, Yurigang, Tosanamita, and Samchunbujo-Oshipsamui. Tae-gon Kim, *The Myths of Korean Shamanism*, 75.

47. Or medicine flowers in some other version. Ibid., 30.

48. Carl G. Jung, *C. G. Jung*, C. W. vol.17, *The Development of Personality*, 176.

49. Ibid., 183.

50. Ann Belford Ulanov, "The Psychological Reality of the Demonic," *Picturing God*, 132-133.

51. Dong-shik Ryu, *The History and Structure of Korean Shamanism*, 314-315.

52. Kwang-sun Suh, *Essays on Korean Heritage and Christianity*, 67.

53. Heu-wan Chae, *Dance of Community and of Joy* (Seoul: Hangilsa, 1985), 46-47.

54. Yul-Kyu Kim, *The Ore of Han and the Stream of Won*, 43-47.

55. Hun-young Im, "The Literature of Han and Minjung Consciousness," *Today's Book* (Seoul: Hangilsa, 1984), 90.

56. Gil-sung Choi, *Shaman in Korea* (Seoul: Yulhwadang, 1981), 220.

57. Bou-yong Rhie, *The Lost Shadow* (Seoul: Jungwoosa, 1983), 153.

58. The Shaman initiation ritual performed in "Hwanghae-do," the North-West Province of Korea. Lucy Hwang, *The "Kut" and Shaman in Korea* (Seoul: Mooneumsa, 1988), 34.

59. The name "naerim-kut" is used for both the whole eighteen rituals and just one of them.

60. Ibid., 34.

61. In case of a ritual for those who died before marriage, a wedding ceremony is performed as the way to resolve the han; a marriage is provided instead of food. These practices are based on the common folk belief that han is generated by ungratified instinctual desire. Gil-sung Choi, *Shaman in Korea*, 148-149.

62. Lucy Hwang, *The Kut and Shaman in Korea*, 34.

63. Bou-yong Rhie, "The Folk Treatment of Mental Illness Among

Shamanistic Society in Korea: Folkpsychiatry in Korea" (11), *Recent Psychiatry* vol.15, No.2 (1972), 71.

64. Chi-ha Kim, one of the minjung poets, played a leading role in the early phase of the Minjung Movement in Korea in 1970's. Chi-ha Kim, *The Southern Land and Boat Songs* (Seoul: Dooreh, 1985), 49-56.

65. An example in the West of "dan" can be found in Martin Luther King Jr's philosophy of non-violence.

66. Carl G. Jung, *C. G. Jung*, C.W. vol.5, 354.

67. Wilfried Daim, *Depth Psychology and Salvation*, trans. Kurt F. Reinhardt (New York: F. Ungar Publishing Co., 1963), 200.

68. Chi-ha Kim. *The Southern Land and Boat Songs*, 53.

69. Ann & Barry Ulanov, *Religion and the Unconscious* (Philadelphia: The Westminster Press, 1975), 205.

70. Lucy Hwang, *The "Kut" and Shaman In Korea*, 33-35.

71. Ibid., 39.

72. Ibid., 40.

73. Carl G. Jung, *C. G. Jung*, C.W. vol.9.1, *The Archetypes and the Collective Unconscious*, 14-15.

74. Kwang-il Kim, *The Psychoanalysis of Korean Traditional Culture*, 353-354.

75. Lucy Hwang, *The "Kut" and Shaman in Korea*, 44-45.

76. Bou-yong Rhie, "Folk Treatment of the Mental Illness Among Shamanistic Society in Korea: Folkpsychiatry in Korea" (11), *The Recent Psychiatry* vol.15, No.2 (Seoul:1972), 71.

Chapter VI

1. Kwang-sun Suh, "Minjung and Theology in Korea: A Biographical Sketch of an Asian Theological Consultation," *Minjung Theology* ed. Yong-bock Kim (Singapore: CTC-CCA Publication, 1981), 17.

2. Hee-suk Moon, *A Korean Minjung Theology: An Old Testament Perspective* (Maryknoll, N.Y. and Hongkong: Orbis Books and Plough Publication, 1985), 1.

3. Yong-bock Kim, "The Socio-Biography of Minjung and Theology," *Minjung and Korean Theology*, ed. The Committee of Theological Study of N.C.C. (Seoul: Korea Theological Study Institute, 1982), 371.

4. Byung-mu Ahn identifies "minjung" with the "ochlos," who were despised, marginalized people in the Gospel Mark in Jesus' time. They are distinguished from the "laos," the lay people in general meaning. "Jesus and Ochlos," *Minjung and Korean Theology*, 89.

5. Minjung theology emerged as part and parcel of the minjung movement along with the emergence of minjung literature, minjung art, and minjung sociology. Tai-il Chun's self-immolation is the momentum of the beginning of Minjung Theology as well as minjung movement. Interview with Byung-mu Ahn. Nov. 10th, 1989.

6. Nam-dong Suh, *Minjung Theology*, 51-52.

7. Dong-hwan Moon, "Korean Minjung Theology," unpublished manuscript, 1980, 5.

8. Nam-dong Suh, *Minjung Theology*, 65.

9. Young-hak Hyun, "A Theological Look at the Mask Dance in Korea, "Minjung Theology," *Minjung Theology*, 43-51.

10. Dong-hwan Moon, "Korean Minjung Theology," 4.

11. Kwang-sun Suh, *Minjung Theology*, 28.

12. Nam-dong Suh, *Minjung Theology*, 60.

13. Ibid., 65.

14. For example, Tae-il Chun, Miss Kyung-sook Kim, Chi-ha Kim, and the heroes and heroines in the literary works of contemporary writers.

15. Nam-dong Suh, Minjung Theology, 52.

16. Ibid.

17. This insight is Yong-bock Kim's main contribution to Minjung theology. See his article "The Socio-biography of Minjung and Theology," *Minjung and Korean Theology*, 369-389.

18. People who are under the rule and control of a sovereign.

19. Nam-dong Suh, *Minjung Theology*, 54.

20. Kwang-sun Suh, *Minjung Theology*, 28.

21. Ibid.

22. Quoted from Nam-dong Suh, *Minjung Theology*, 60-61.

23. Nam-dong Suh, *Minjung Theology*, 60.

24. Dong-hwan Moon, "Korean Minjung Theology," 5.

25. Young-hak Hyun, "A Theological Look at the Mask Dance in Korea," *Minjung Theology*, 48.

26. Quoted from Nam-dong Suh, "The Life of the World and Christ," *The Exploration of Minjung Theology*, 352-353.

27. Ibid., 353.

28. Kwang-sun Suh, *Minjung Theology*, 19.

29. Ibid., 27.

30. Nam-dong Suh, *Minjung Theology*, 54.

31. Quoted from Jung Young Lee's translation. *An Emerging Theology in World Perspective: Commentary on Korean Minjung Theology*, 155-156.

2. Yushin Yoo, *Korea The Beautiful; Treasure of the Hermit Kingdom* (Seoul: Samsung Moonhwa Printing Co., 1987), 192.

33. Yul-kyu Kim, *The Ore of Han and the Stream of Won* (Seoul: Joowoosa, 1981), 145.

34. Nam-dong Suh, *Minjung Theology*, 58.

35. Ibid., 55.

36. Kwang-sun Suh, *Minjung Theology*, 28.

37. Byung-mu Ahn, *The Story of Minjung Theology*, (Seoul: Korea Theological Study Institute, 1988), 208.

38. Carl G. Jung, *C. G. Jung*, C.W. vol.8, *The Structure and Dynamics of the Psyche* (Princeton: Princeton University Press, 1964), 217.

39. Dong-hwan Moon, "Korean Minjung Theology," 6-7.

40. Ibid., 7.

41. According to Melanie Klein greed is one of the derivatives of envy, but it is not as much destructive as envy. Klein explains, greed is an insatiable craving, exceeding what the subject needs and what the object is able to give. At the unconscious level, greed aims primarily at completely scooping out, sucking dry, and devouring the breast: its aims is to destructive introjection; whereas envy not only seeks to rob in this way, but also to put badness into the mother in order to spoil and destroy her. Melanie Klein, *Envy and Gratitude and Other Works* (New York: The Free Press, 1975), 181.

42. Quoted from Nam-dong Suh. *Minjung Theology*, 61.

43. Quoted from Dong-hwan Moon, "Korean Minjung theology," 7.

44. Quoted from Nam-dong Suh. *Minjung Theology*, 61.

45. Chi-ha Kim, *Southern Land and Its Boat Songs*, 53.

46. Nam-dong Suh, *Minjung Theology*, 61-62.

47. Chi-ha Kim, *Southern Land and Its Boat Songs* (Seoul: Dooreh, 1985), 50-51.

48. Ibid., 48.

49. Ibid., 55.

50. When Chu-yong returned home from outside in the night he saw a man sleeping in the bed with his wife. This man in fact was an evil spirit trying to test Chu-yong's integrity. Instead of confronting the evil man Chu-yong sang a song while dancing. Quoted from Bou-yong Rhie, "Dealing with Evil in Korean Fairytales," *Korea Journal* (Seoul: January 1980), 24.

51. For example, the story of "Kongjui-Patjui" and "Bari-Kongjoo."

52. See Chapter V.

53. Carl G. Jung, *Symbols of Transformation*, C.W. vol.5. 2nd ed. (Princeton: Princeton University Press, 1967), 305.

54. Chi-ha Kim, *Southern Land and Its Boat Songs*, 52.

55. In the period of 1984 and 1985, Chi-ha Kim wrote "A New Understanding of Life and the Practice of Cooperative Life" and "At the Valley of "Kuri" in which the birth of the new Chi-ha Kim is heralded. Especially in the later article, he extensively discusses the unification of the feminine and masculine principles.

56. See Ann Belford Ulanov, "Stages of Anima Development," *The Feminine in Jungian Psychology and in Christian Theology.* (Evanston: North Western University Press, 1971), 212-240.

57. Nam-dong Suh, *Minjung Theology* (Singapore: CTC-CCA Publication, 1981), 65.

58. Chi-ha Kim, *Southern Land and Its Boat Songs* (Seoul: Dooreh, 1985), 55.

Bibliography

Primary Sources

Ahn Byung-mu. [*Stories of Minjung Theology*]. Seoul: Korea Theological Study Institute, 1988.

Chae Heu-wan. [*Dance of Community and Joy*]. Seoul: Hangilsa, 1985.

The Committee of National History Publication. [*Korean History*]. vol.9, Seoul: Tamgoodang, 1974.

Guntrip Harry. Schizoid Phenomena, *Object Relations and the Self*. New York: International Universities Press, Inc., 1969.

Hankuk Institute of Theology. ed. [*Discussions on Korean Minjung*]. Seoul: Korea Theological Study Institute, 1984.

Hwang Lucy. [*Korean Shamans and Their Ritual*]. Seoul: Mooneumsa, 1988.

Im Hun-young. "Literature of Han and the Consciousness of People." [*Books Today*]. Seoul: Hangilsa, 1984.

Jung Carl Gustav. "The Synthetic or Constructive Method." (1917) The Collected Works of C. G. Jung. Edited by William Mcguire. Translated by R. F. C. Hull. 2nd ed. Bollingen Series 20, vol.7, *Two Essays on Analytical Psychology*. Princeton: Princeton University Press, 1953. "Individuation." (1917) "The Development of Personality." (1934) The Collected Works of C. G. Jung. vol.17, *The Development of Personality*.

"A Study in the Process of Individuation." (1950) "Archetypes of the Collective Unconscious." (1954) The Collected Works of C. G. Jung vol.9.1, *The Archetypes and the Collective Unconscious*.

"The Self." (1948) The Collected Works of C. G. Jung vol. 9.2, *Aion*.

"A Review of the Complex Theory." (1948) "On the Nature of the Psyche." (1954)

"The Conjunction." (1956) The Collected Works of C. G. Jung. vol.14, *Mysterium Coniunctionis.*

Jung Carl G., von Franz Marie-Louise, Henderson Joseph L., Jacobi Jolande, Jaffe' Aniela. *Man and His Symbols.* New York: Dell Publishing Co., Inc., 1968.

Kim Chi-ha. [*Southern Land Boat-Songs*]. Seoul: Dooreh, 1985.

Kim Harvey Yong-sook. *Six Korean Women.* Minnesota: West Publishing Co., 1979.

Kim Kwang-il. [*Psychoanalysis of Korean Traditional Culture*]. Seoul: Siensa, 1984.

Kim Tae-gon. [*A Study of Korean Shamanism*]. Seoul: Jipmoondang, 1981. [*Myth of Korean Shamanism*]. Seoul: Jipmoondang, 1985.

Kim Yong-bock. ed. *Minjung Theology.* Singapore: A CTC-CCA Publication, 1981.

Kim Yul-kyu. [*The Ore of Han and the Stream of "Won"*]. Seoul: Joowoo, 1981.

[*Korean Myth, Folk Beliefs, Folklore*]. Seoul: Jungeumsa, 1983.

Klein Melanie. "The Psychological Foundations of Child Analysis." (1926) "The Technique of Early Analysis." (1926) "Early Stages of the Oedipus Conflict and of Super-Ego Formation." (1928) "The Significance of Early Anxiety Situations in the Development of the Ego." (1929) *The Psychoanalysis of Children*, Translated by Alix Strachey. Seymour Lawrence: Delacorte Press, 1975. "Infantile Anxiety Situations Reflected in a Work of Art and in the Creative Impulse." (1929) "The Importance of Symbol-Formation in the Development of the Ego." (1930) "The Early Development of Conscience in the Child." (1933) "A Contribution to the Psychogenesis of Manic-Depressive States." (1935) "Love, Guilt, and Reparation." (1937) "Mourning and its Relation to Manic-Depressive States." (1940) *Love, Guilt and Reparation and Other Works.* New York: Dell Publishing Co., Inc., 1975. "Notes on Some Schizoid Mechanisms." (1946) "On the Theory of Anxiety and Guilt." (1948) "Envy and Gratitude." (1957) *Envy and Gratitude & Other Works.* New York: Dell Publishing Co., Inc., 1975.

Ko Eun, [*Being Transformed, Where Shall We Meet?*]. Seoul: Choongang Press, 1971.

[*For Disillusion*]. Seoul: Mineumsa, 1977.

[*Poetry and Reality*]. Seoul: Silchunmoonhaksa, 1986.

[*Son of Red-Soil: My Childhood*]. Seoul: Hangilsa, 1986.

[*The Peak of the Wind*]. Seoul: Nanam, 1987.

[*The Sound of My Wave*]. Seoul: Nanam, 1987.

Korean History Research Association. [*Korean History in Story Telling*]. Seoul: Chungah Press, 1987.

Korea Publishing Institute. [*The History of Korea*]. vol.8, Seoul: Shinhwa Press, 1974.

Kyunghee University Institute of Folk Study. [*Korean Folk-Tradition*]. Seoul: Siensa, 1986.

Lee Jung-young. ed. *An Emerging Theology in World Perspective: Commentary on Korean Minjung Theology*. Mystic: Twenty-third Publications, 1988.

Lee Kyu-tae. [*The History of Korean Folklore*]. vol.2. Seoul: Hyuneumsa, 1983.

Lee Sang-hyun. ed. *Essays on Korean Heritage and Christianity*. Princeton Junction: The Association of Korean Christian Scholars in North America, Inc., 1984.

Moon Dong-hwan. "Korean Minjung Theology." New York: Union Theological Seminary, 1981. Unpublished manuscript photocopied.

The National Culture Association. [*Yun-Ryu-Sil-Ki-Sul*]. Seoul: Kwangmyung, 1966.

Rhie Bou-yong. [*Analytical Psychology*]. Seoul: Iljokag, 1978. "Dealing with Evil in Korean Fairytales: A Psychological Implication." *Korea Journal* (January, 1980).

"Illness and Healing in the Three Kingdoms Period: A Symbolical Interpretation." *Korea Journal* (December, 1981).

[*The Lost Shadow*]. Seoul: Jungwoosa, 1983.

"A Study on the Korean Folk Healing of Mental Illness." [*Recent Psychiatry*]. (No.2. 1972).

Ryu Dong-sik. [*The History and Structure of the Korean Shamanism*]. Seoul: Yonsei University Press, 1975.

Suh Chang-won. "A Formulation of Minjung Theology: Toward a Socio-historical Theology of Asia." Unpublished Ph. D. Thesis, Union Theological Seminary (N.Y., N.Y.). 1986.

Suh Nam-dong. [*Theology at a Turning Point*]. Seoul: Korea Theological Study Institute. 1976.

"A Counter-Theological Consideration of the Korean Folklore." [*History and Existence: Essays written in the celebration of Dr. Byung-mu Ahn's 60th birthday*]. Seoul: The Christian Literature Society. 1982.

"A Confluence of the Two Stories." [*Minjung and the Korean Theology*] ed. by The Committee of Theological Study of K.N.C.C. Seoul: Korea Theological Study Institute. 1982.

"The Priest of Han." "The Symbol-Formation of Han and a Theological Reflection." [*The Exploration of Minjung Theology*]. Seoul: Hangilsa, 1983.

Ulanov Ann Belford. *The Feminine In Jungian Psychology and in Christian Theology*. Evanston: Northwestern University Press, 1971.

Picturing God. New York: Cowley Publication, 1986.

Ulanov Ann Belford and Ulanov Barry. *Religion and the Unconscious*. Philadelphia: The Westminster Press, 1975.

Cinderella and Her Sisters: The Envy and the Envying. Philadelphia: The Westminster Press, 1983.

Winnicott D. W.. *The Maturational Processes and the Facilitating Environment*. New York: International Universities Press, Inc., 1965.

Secondary Sources

Gross Kurth Phyllis. *Melanie Klein: Her World and Her Work*. Cambridge: Harvard University Press, 1987.

Im Hun-young and Yoon Koo-byung. ed. [*Kim Chi-ha: His Literature and Thoughts*]. Seoul: Sekye, 1984.

Jacobi Jolande. *The Psychology of Jung*. Translated by Ralph Manheim. New York: Pantheon, 1959.

Segal Hanna. *Introduction to the Work of Melanie Klein*. New York: Basic Books, Inc., 1964.

Melanie Klein. New York: Viking Press, 1978.